VOICES
OF IRELAND

*I dedicate this book to
the real people of my Highways and Byways
without whom I would feel incomplete*

*Donncha O Dúlaing records his appreciation
to the Bank of Ireland
for their support in the publication of Voices of Ireland.
Buíochas mór dóibh.*

VOICES
OF IRELAND

Conversations with

DONNCHA
O DULAING

Biographies by Henry Boylan

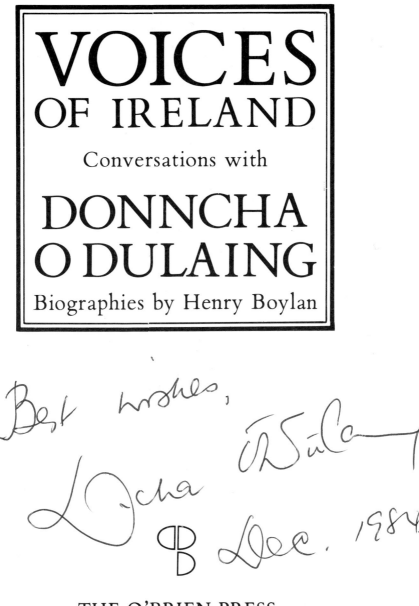

Best wishes,

Dcha O Dulaing

Dec. 1984

THE O'BRIEN PRESS
in association with
RTE

First Published 1984
The O'Brien Press Ltd.
20 Victoria Road, Dublin 6, Ireland.
in association with
Radio Telefís Éireann (RTE)

British Library Cataloguing in Publication Data

O Dúlaing, Donncha
Voices of Ireland
1. Ireland — Social life and custom — 20th century
I. Title
941.70824   D. 959.1

ISBN 0-86278-063-2 HB
ISBN 0-86278-065-9 PB

Editor: Íde ní Laoghaire
Cover Design: Frank Spiers
Book Design: Michael O'Brien
Typeset in Bembo by: Inset Ltd.
Printing: Leinster Leader, Naas

Contents

Introduction

Daniel Corkery, in the introduction to *The Hidden Ireland*, has an invaluable piece of advice for anyone who may wish to discover the real Ireland: 'To reach it one must, leaving the cities and towns behind, venture among the bogs and hills, far into the mountains. . . .' William Bulfin, in the first chapter of *Rambles in Eirinn*, is writing of the same country, the same people: 'This land of ours revels in beauty. She is a favoured child of nature; and I pity anyone born of her who would not prefer her loveliness to that of any other land, for it is second to none!'

Both Corkery and Bulfin adequately and eloquently express all that I might feel of Ireland and its people. These beliefs have been borne in on me by almost twenty years of travelling, on foot, in pony and trap, and by car, through every county. During the radio life of my beloved 'Highways and Byways', there is hardly a ribbon of road, hardly a range of hills, hardly a village or town, which has not offered me friendship and hospitality.

The people of the hidden Ireland and the people of the public Ireland have generously presented me with favours the like of which any one man is ill-equipped to repay. They have spoken to me of the Ireland that I love. They have spoken at times warmly, at others sadly, but always with that genuine ring of truth which comes from people who live close to reality. These are my voices of Ireland and among them are the people you will meet between the covers of this book.

Curiously enough, the 'voices' herein meet together accidentally. I never had any intention of joining Mick Mackey with Siobhán McKenna, Eamon de Valera with Edna O'Brien, Micheál macLiammóir with Nora Connolly-O'Brien or Leslie Bean de Barra with Paschal McGuinness. Yet, their very disparateness unites them, for they are, in many and varied ways, public voices of the hidden Ireland.

My life is bound up with meetings, meetings with people,

and, to the best of my ability, I have striven to present these people exactly as I found them. They have been good to me, so I have always tried to be fair to them. I learned early on that the Ireland of 'Highways and Byways' was a homely place and that I was constantly enriched by discovering it. So it is with these voices. Their authenticity, their ease of expression, has been actively and deliberately fostered by the fact that each of my subjects is at home. The only imposition, microphone and tape-recorder, is obscured by a naturalness, an unaffected truth, far removed from the trendy artificiality of a recording studio.

Séamus Murphy talked to me as he looked lovingly at the heads of his friends in his workshop in Blackpool. Micheál macLiammóir was comfortable by his fireside when this, his last interview, was recorded. Nora Connolly-O'Brien recalled the heroic past of 1916 while she 'wet' the tea, and Mick Mackey's hospitable wife Kitty, interrupted heroic talk of hurling and hurling men to offer Mick and myself the flaithiúlacht of their Ardnacrusha home. Siobhán McKenna talked tenderly of her early Abbey days in the hypnotic and gentle stillness of her Dublin home, while Eamon de Valera unfolded the stories of his boyhood at his presidential home in Aras an Uachtaráin.

These 'voices' represent a certain immutability. We will never see their kind again. There was but one Eamon de Valera from Bruree. The son that old Pat Peyton reared and then sent abroad, is unique. MacLiammóir, the Irish Renaissance man, supped at the table of genius. Siobhán McKenna is the very embodiment of the Irish theatre. Leslie Bean de Barra is of that type of unique Irishwoman born for 1916 and for the noblest service to the nation. Mick Mackey, well, Mick Mackey is Mick Mackey!

Many of my friends in this book have helped to make and shape the story of our nation. Whether in literature, theatre, sculpture, religion, politics or revolution, their voices are clear and distinct. I owe an incalculable debt to each. Without them, my life would be incomplete. They have enriched us all.

Donncha O Dúlaing

Eamon de Valera speaks to the crowd at Ennis on his first election campaign, 1918.

Eamon de Valera

I always hoped that some day I would meet Eamon de Valera. Dev, as he was called, more than any other historical figure had dominated my Charleville boyhood. Every day when I went to school at the Christian Brothers I saw his picture as he stood, solemn among his peers, in his far-off schooldays. Then, too, I often cycled from Charleville to Bruree and passed by the de Valera family home at Knockmore. Again, my earliest political memory is of a night when Dev and Seán Moylan came to Charleville for a political meeting. They were received with flaming tar barrels, torches and cheers and I climbed up the side of the lorry and got close enough to the 'Chief' to shake his hand. I still remember the austere look and the undiluted county Limerick accent of the man who was at once a distant mystery and a close connection for all of us who grew up in Charleville in the forties and fifties.

When I joined Radio Éireann in 1964 it was a certainty that 'A Munster Journal', which I produced and presented in the Cork studios, would have a north Cork and south Limerick bias. It was certain too, that I would sooner or later, visit the home of Mainchín Seoighe, the writer and chronicler of all things Irish, at his home in Tankardstown, near Bruree, in the county of Limerick. I did. His mother, Mrs. Nora Joyce, had been a schoolmate of Eamon de Valera's in Bruree and even referred to him, affectionately and to his face, as 'Dev' and 'Eddie'. The President often called to see her. Wouldn't it be nice to meet him?

One morning in the late spring of 1965 Mainchin rang me to say that Dev would be paying a private visit to Bruree in early October. There was a long pause at my end of the phone. He asked if I would like to be there - 'quite unofficially, of course.' I would.

So it was that on a grey, misty, unpromising, nervous morning I, the unknown newcomer to broadcasting, arrived at the Joyce home hoping to secure the scoop of my life. It was like the morning of a station Mass! All quiet! All excited! All spic, span, and waiting. I sat, walked, wished and waited from nine o'clock in the morning until the late afternoon. By that time my nerves were screaming and my courage had almost evaporated.

Mainchin's sister Mary suddenly called out, 'He's outside.' There was a flurry of introductions and Mainchin introduced me to Máire Ní Cheallaigh, the President's private secretary, who in turn introduced me to the great man. 'Oh,' he said quietly, 'Donncha O Dúlaing, bhfuil Gaeilge agat?' Bhí agus fáilte. 'Cá rabhais ar scoil?' Here was a glimmer of hope. 'Rathluirc.' 'Chuadhas féin ann,' he said. Then he asked, 'Cá bhfuairis do chuid Gaeilge?' And added, 'Os na bráithre, cosúil liom féin? Bhí siad ar fheabhas mar mhúinteoirí nuair a bhíos ar scoil ann.'

I felt that I was winning and that I had a chance of talking at length with him. Máire Ní Cheallaigh outlined my wishes to the Chief: 'He'd like to broadcast a programme about your childhood.' 'Oh yes,' he said, 'and what is so special about me? I went to the national school in Bruree, then on to the Brothers in Rathluirc like everyone else.' There was a question mark in the statement. 'Well,' I said with great temerity, 'you were the only one to become President.' He smiled, but only just. Then, 'Cad is féidir liom a dhéanamh ar do shon?'

With a rush I explained that I had with me all the facilities to record a long conversation. He raised his hand, 'No, we must not do it now. This is too unexpected.' And for the next hour he regaled me with the magic I sought as he trod and re-trod his well-loved 'bóithrín na smaointe', the days of his boyhood.

The frustration was almost unbearable. Here was the stuff of dreams, given with generosity and lost as soon as it was uttered! Would I ever record him?

To make a long story short, there were phone calls to Bruree and Aras an Uachtaráin, letters to and from Máire Ní Cheallaigh and journeys to record many of the President's old schoolmates. Finally the great day dawned and I arrived at the Aras. It was time to record history and to realise a boyhood ambition - to speak to Eamon de Valera, a boy from Bruree, and record his unique story.

 DEV: We landed at Queenstown [Cobh] and then went by train to Kilmallock. At the station we were met - my uncle Ed was with me - we were met at the station by his brother, my uncle Pat. He had, probably, a donkey and cart to take the luggage.

DONNCHA: What are your first actual memories of Knockmore?

DEV: My first night there, curiously enough, was the last night that anybody slept in what we called 'the old house'. The old house was a thatched house. The walls were of mud or clay and they were fairly substantial - I remember using a pickaxe and crowbar in later years to try and break them up and they were about three feet at the base.

My first night, anyhow, was in that old house and I wakened up in the morning and there was nobody about. I suppose I was frightened and I shouted and screamed. At any rate my aunt, who would have been about fifteen years of age at that time, came in to soothe me and I asked her where Uncle Ed was and she told me that he was up at the new house. I

*Dev, aged four, wearing his aunt's boots for his first
photograph, 1886.*

remember wondering what the new house could be. 'Twas a cottage - I remember it well. I was always interested in the fact that my first night in Ireland was the last night that anybody slept in the old house.

DONNCHA: Were you made to feel at home around Bruree?

DEV: The curious thing is I seemed to have the entrance to every house in the neighbourhood. I knew them and would walk in quite easily.

DONNCHA: Did the people around Bruree have any special characteristics?

DEV: Well, they must have been a friendly people because I was always made feel at home in any of the houses on my routes, that is around by Howardstown and so on.

DONNCHA: Did your boyhood around Bruree colour your life afterwards?

DEV: I'm certain that I was greatly influenced by all I heard in the neighbourhood and by the contacts I made as a boy.

DONNCHA: Do you remember at all, a Uachtaráin, when you had your first photograph taken?

DEV: Oh, I remember it well. I think it was when my aunt was about to go to America and they were anxious to send my photograph to my mother. So, I had a grand journey to Limerick by train. Of course I was dolled up before I started out! One of the problems was the boots; apparently they didn't pass muster. A solution was found - they found that my aunt's button boots would fit me. At least *they* thought so! I didn't like the idea at all! I would have preferred my old boots. However, they fitted on my aunt's boots and I was taken to O'Shea's of Limerick and I remember seeing the man behind the cover which he put on his head when he was taking the photograph and he was trying to attract my attention so that I would look straight at him. I have a copy of the photograph still.

DONNCHA: It's over eighty years now, a Uachtaráin, since you first picked up a book, yet you still remember an alphabet book sent to you from America by your mother. Could you recite?

DEV: A is for ape who has four clever hands,
he lives in the woods in the tropical lands.
B is for boar, a savage wild pig,
with his terrible tusks for roots he can dig.
C is for cat who is fond of the house
and very much likes to run after a mouse.
D is for donkey, a mild, patient beast,
who thinks some fresh thistles a very great feast.
E is for elephant, of mighty great size,
kind to all children and gentle and wise.
F is for fox whose home's in the ground,
and often is chased by huntsman and hound.
Ní cuimhin liom 'G'. Tá mé cinnte nach 'goat' a bhí ann.
H is for horse, man's greatest friend . . .
is ní féidir liom deire a chur leis!
I is for ibex, a goat with long horns,
he lives in the highlands, the lowlands he scorns.
J is for jaguar, a fierce beast of prey,
who hides in America's forests by day.
K is for kangaroo, upright he keeps,
something, something - he leaps!
L is for lynx . . .
Ní cuimhin liom a thuille.

* * *

DONNCHA: Do you remember your first day at school?
DEV: I can't say that I remember exactly coming into the school or what happened on that first day, but I do remember the schoolroom very well. It has been divided since, unfortunately. It was a fine room as it was and there would be about sixty pupils. One half would be, as a rule, standing up and the other half would be sitting down in the desks. Those who would be in the desks would be writing or doing some arithmetical exercises, or, perhaps, learning grammar. Those who were standing were being questioned or taught directly by the teachers. I remember well in the winter time, on one

De Valera's mother, Catherine.

occasion anyway, we had to bring one shilling each to buy coal, so that if even half the class brought it, it would bring us through the winter.

DONNCHA: I know that you had a great interest in geography and there was, I believe, a game associated with it that you and your schoolfriends played in the school in Bruree.

DEV: That was a game we had for those of us who got in early in the morning before the master came. We'd stand around in front of a map of the world and try to puzzle each other by asking such strange questions as, Point out Kamaskatka!, Point out Christmas Island!, and so on.

DONNCHA: I gather that globes also held an attraction for you.

DEV: Yes. We had two very fine globes, one a terrestrial globe and the other a celestial one. I never bothered much about the celestial one - I'm wondering why I didn't.

The only map that I have a distinct recollection of was a map of the world with the two hemispheres shown on it - it was not like the Mercator projection map which I saw in Lloyd George's room when I went to see him. He had it in front of me and a great part of the world was coloured red [the British Empire]!

DONNCHA: People at this time often travelled long distances to work and I suppose the pupils and teachers of Bruree were no exception. You once talked to me of a teacher, a Mr Paddy Kelly?

DEV: I remember him coming in on a bicycle with a big wheel and a small wheel — I saw a race once in Bruree on penny farthings. The great thing was that there was a step up to the small wheel. So they started the race standing, with their hands on the handlebars and they had to climb up and start off and it was very interesting to watch them.

DONNCHA: Tell me, did the young boys ever smoke going or coming from school?

DEV: Oh, yes. Ratan. There's a certain cane and it's very porous and if you burn it you can suck the smoke through it, and we called it ratan. I don't know what is the real name for it. If there was a small one of these ratan canes we'd use it.

Turf was very common too. We smoked turf and this chap Mortell - 'twas he introduced me to the lucky bag, a penny lucky bag, and in this lucky bag one of the things you'd be hoping to get was a little pipe, but you'd put turf in it. Although, I heard that some people used tea!

DONNCHA: What games did you play?

DEV: There was a slight slope in the school yard and sometimes we used to get geosadáns [thistles]! Now, you can easily pull it up and the geosadán has a good healthy root to it. So we used to have battles. Those who went down Howardstown way at the Cross of the Pump, we were in one batch, against those who went over towards Joyce's country, that's in the Tankardstown direction.

We arranged to have a fight in the school yard on this particular day at lunchtime and we all armed ourselves in Roche's field with geosadáns. I was at the lower end, defending against the hill. I wasn't by any means a leader! There was a charge and in the charge I was thrown back and a fellow put a broken tip of a shoe through the palm of my hand. I have the mark to this present day.

DONNCHA: You had a friend called Jack Potter?

DEV: Jack Potter! He used to come to school on a donkey with a beautiful leather saddle. I used to envy him, of course, with his beautiful saddle. I had only an old sack.

My uncle used to invite him in to read. He used to read very well. I remember, 'twas in the second book [second class], my uncle used to hold him up as a model to me always. 'Why don't you be like Jack Potter?' But, I'm afraid that I wasn't able to come to his state of excellence at all, according to my uncle.

DONNCHA: There is a nice twist to the Jack Potter story.

DEV: Oh yes, indeed there is! I had the measles and I was in the little bedroom from which you could see the kitchen table. Jack Potter came in and my grandmother was around. It was a day on which there was an examination. My grandmother said to Jack that as I had measles I wouldn't be going to the exam. 'That's right, Mrs Coll,' says he, 'measles are dangerous things. When you have the measles, 'tis very dangerous to go out.' I heard this in bed and I thought 'twas the ruse of a chap who was very interested in keeping me in bed, so, as there had been a bit of rivalry because of my uncle holding him up as a model and because of the fact that if you hadn't passed the exam you wouldn't be promoted – I didn't want that – I slipped out the window.

I'd like to measure the window, because it is a small window and how in the name of heavens I ever got out I don't know!

DONNCHA: Was there any mitching from school in those days?

DEV: Oh yes! There was a word that you probably wouldn't understand: 'leaching', and 'slinging', two words to describe mitching.

Dick Coll wasn't in on this particular day so the master asked me to go and bring him in! It was an afternoon off for me and like most kids I was delighted to get away from the books and went off to bring in Dick. I went to his house and asked was he about and I met a man who used to sell tea – he had a pony and trap and took tea around and used to sell it to the various people. He had a very good voice. One of the songs he sang was 'The Man Who Broke the Bank in Monte Carlo'. We called him Monte Carlo. He used to be singing as he drove along. Monte Carlo asked me, 'Who do you want?' 'I want Dick,' I said. 'Oh, I think he's in the barn,' he said. So, he got me into the barn and he locked me in. I have an idea that I climbed up to a window again and got out! That was my first imprisonment. He used to always boast that he was my first jailor!

*   *   *

DONNCHA: Later you went to school in Charleville. How did you travel from Knockmóre?

DEV: I went by train in the morning. I had to get up very early. The train left Bruree about twenty minutes to eight o'clock. I suppose it reached Charleville station about eight o'clock and then I walked in the mile and a half from the station to the school. I got into the school roughly before nine o'clock and I utilised any time I had in the train to make up my home lessons. That was the only time I had to do this except at weekends.

DONNCHA: Were the trains very comfortable?

DEV: Oh, I didn't bother about comfort at that time. Looking back, I know that there were no cushions on the seats - we were travelling third class. What interested me most was our own station in Bruree. It was a favourite playground of mine with some of the other boys. We used to go up to Sutton's store and when the wagons were emptied of the coal they were allowed to slide down to the buffers on a slope. We used to be always anxious to get a jaunt on them on these occasions. We would cling on to the side of the truck and stand on the brake when we wanted to bring it to a halt.

DONNCHA: The daily journey home must have been a drudgery at times, but were there pleasant times too?

DEV: Once when we were coming home as usual a chap named Willie Daly came along on a horse. He had obviously taken too much to drink because he was going from side to side. I knew the man well. He had a famous horse, March Boy, and it was this horse he was riding. It was a horse that had won the Charleville Plate and he had great regard for it. I was afraid that he'd tumble off and get killed because just at our house a man had fallen from a horse and was unconscious for a long time. So, I was anxious about him but I could do nothing.

Then John Gubbins came along with his steward, Armstrong, shortly after. When he caught up with the horseman he stopped and the steward pulled the man off the horse and this man was kicking very hard. He didn't want to be moved from his horse but the steward was a big strong man and he lifted him up on Mr Gubbins's sidecar and put him sitting alongside him.

Then, the horse was in question - what were they going to do with the horse? It was hard enough to keep this man quiet, but to bring the horse was another matter. So, Gubbins saw us coming along and he beckoned. He said, 'Can any of you ride a horse?' So, I put up my hand. I could! I had ridden horses for farmers around but I had never been on a racehorse before. I got on the horse and then we were going to trot after the car. But whenever I was near the car the owner of the horse became obstreperous and they had difficulty with him. So, they beckoned me to go back. I was delighted. I turned around and I cantered back half a mile and then cantered back half a mile again until I came near them and cantered back again. I had a great time.

*   *   *

DONNCHA: Was there any unhappiness in your boyhood?
DEV: I was digging potatoes and this boy Mortell, I had heard that he was going to Limerick to learn the grocery business and that meant my nearest companion going from me. It made me thoughtful. I remember saying to myself, I suppose I have to keep on digging potatoes for the rest of my life!
DONNCHA: Would you say that Bruree is the linchpin of your childhood?
DEV: Yes. I tell you I had to study a book of Miss Mitford called *Our Village*. I often thought while I was doing it, even at school, how one could write on our village. I wasn't, however, sufficiently intimate with the life of our village to pick out the droll characters.

I remember a man named Johnny who used to come by. I remember my uncle used to always see that he had a glass of whiskey going to Mass on Christmas Day when he'd be passing by. The whiskey they'd have got as presents from the grocers.

I remember going to the village on Christmas Night for the Christmas groceries with my grandmother. I remember the first creamery butter I'd ever seen, a pound of creamery butter. I'd seen butter churned, of course. My grandmother would churn when we wanted butter for ourselves, but it was never as nice looking as this creamery butter! So she'd go in to buy the sugar and the tea. Generally she'd buy the sugar by the stone and a pound of tea, or a half-stone of sugar if she hadn't

*De Valera's uncle, Pat Coll, with whom he spent much
of his childhood.*

enough money. One of the shops was owned by a woman named O'Donoghue, she had a shop at the corner opposite the church and they'd give you a great big Christmas cake and you usually got a bottle of whiskey and usually a bottle of wine, port wine. Very nice stuff to taste!

I remember well now the Christmas Eve with the white cloth on the table. It was a festive occasion. The Christmas candle was lit in the window and I was generally given the privilege of lighting the candle.

On Easter Sunday I remember I used to be brought out to see the sun dancing. I saw no sun dancing. I was terribly disappointed!

DONNCHA: Which was your favourite boyhood haunt around Knockmore? Was there any place where you liked to be alone?

DEV: Oh, the whole area! The hill of Knockmore, the hill of Knockfenora and then down by the brook, the old moat. There was a very nice hazel tree, where you'd get hazel nuts in the autumn. There were other places I knew over in Clonbrien where you'd get the finest sloes in the country. I used to eat haws too! I found that the haws were pretty good.

*   *   *

DONNCHA: In the country everything revolves around the cows - feeding, milking and, often, minding. Was it any different in Knockmore?

DEV: No. That was one of my principal tasks. Very often I had to feed the cows. I remember cutting buckets of turnips for them in the evening and cutting some hay off the bench with a hayknife and giving them, as we'd say, a gabháil [armful] of hay.

My uncle, of course, took principal care of them, but there was only a half-acre attached to the cottage. It wasn't sufficient to feed the cows. We had three or four cows generally and you had to get some pasture for them. The only available pasture was that on the roadside, the broad edges between the road proper and the fences. There was very good grass on them too. There was, of course, plenty of dust on them as well. There was very little traffic. One of my tasks was to take the cows out on the 'long farm', as we called the roadside, and look after them. I had to be particularly careful because you could be summoned at that time by the police for cattle straying on the road. If anyone was with the cattle you could not be so easily summoned because it would be much harder to prove you weren't taking the cattle from one place to another.

My sight was better than that of my uncle so I generally had to look out for the police. I remember I could easily distinguish two policemen. They always went out on their beat in pairs. If they were going in the evening they generally took their carbines, strapped over their shoulders, with their bayonets by their sides. They walked in such a way that it was very obvious to me from a distance, which was probably half a mile away, that they were policemen. When I saw them I went for the cows and drove them off the road which was their [the policemen's] general beat. In that way I used to look after the cows. On Saturdays I'd probably spend the whole day with them. I got to know every blade of grass. I certainly knew nearly every bush on the roadside!

When I was minding the cows, of course, that was when I was able to read. I remember reading *Robinson Crusoe*. Then, later, I used to read books on the hill of Knockfenora. I remember reading a life of Napoleon by Abbott. It's a very full life and he was an admirer of Napoleon's and it was written from a sympathetic point of view. It was very interesting, but a very big book. However, I managed to get through it on the side of the hill of Knockfenora. The books I really remember best are the big books. First of all, the Abbé MacGeoghegan's *History of Ireland* from which my uncle used to read aloud from time to time. Then, we had also *The Scottish Chiefs* and my mother had brought a copy of *Moore's Melodies.* My uncle used to read those. I can see him in recollection, sitting on the table on Sunday afternoons reading aloud the songs from the *Melodies.* And then, in the Uncle Remus Club we got books like *The Bog of Stars,* and *Ivanhoe* which was one of the first books that I remember reading when I was going to the national school, and *The Story of Ireland* of course.

DONNCHA: The country people worked hard at that time but there were, of course, compensations, like visits to the fair in Charleville.

DEV: I used to go with my uncle. One of the ways he had of making a living was he'd buy cattle - young steers - or breed them sometimes, and when they were yearlings he'd have them out on grass: there were people who let out land for grazing. Then you had to bring them to the fair to sell.

My uncle usen't to be able to see very well in the dark. The fair of Charleville was one of the very early morning fairs, so we had to get up very early when 'twas dark, and I used to accompany him when I was strong enough to go out to collect the cattle. And very often I went to the fair because it's always well to have two looking after cattle. I've often stood in the fair of Charleville.

DONNCHA: It must have been a cold stand on a winter's morning?

DEV: Indeed it was. I remember one very bad morning my uncle went across to what's now the Imperial Hotel to get something to eat and drink. We had left without breakfast in the early morning. So, when he went in, he arranged that I could come in after him. The woman was very, very kind. It was very cold. She did her best. She brought me in by the fire in the kitchen and then she got me some bread and butter, I'm sure. I don't remember the bread and butter but I do remember the stout! She got me some brown stout and said, 'Now the best thing to do is to mull this.' So, she put the poker in the fire and got it quite hot and put it in and warmed the stout. I thought 'twas a wonderful drink!

*   *   *

DONNCHA: Did you go to many country funerals?

DEV: The first one that I can remember was that of an old man named Mick Lyons. He was being buried fifteen or sixteen miles from Knockmore. My uncle was going to the funeral. He was in the covered car - as a rule, the hearse was accompanied by a covered car. It was open at the back, with leather curtains which could be pulled aside when the weather was fine or closed across if it was raining.

At the funeral also was a man named Barron. He was riding a chestnut mare which he afterwards entered for some of the races in Charleville. He was a very heavy man and seeing that I was in the covered car he thought it would be better that I, a youngster, should be on the mare's back rather than himself. He spoke to my uncle and an exchange was effected. I, of course, was delighted with myself. I rode the whole way and back again.

I also had an experience with Mr Barron on another occasion. I think 'twas the same horse. I was sent by my uncle to his house to bring back a horse that had been doing some ploughing. When I brought in the plough horse, he said, 'Oh, you are just what I want.' He was putting in the horse for the races in Charleville and he had no lightweight rider. He himself was very heavy and he felt that the horse wasn't getting the sort of experience that it wanted for the race. So, he sent me down a long field, about half a mile in length. I got into the saddle and she went off like a shot, like the wind, and then to my horror in the middle of the field there was a trench. I said, This is the end of me, anyhow! But, to my amazement, she went over it like a bird. I was hardly shaken in the saddle. Then I turned her and, of course, coming back I hadn't any of the fears that I had the first time. I was delighted. The speed was great. To be on the back of a racehorse and to let her go as fast as she could go! She really went!

DONNCHA: Funerals, of course, are very important social occasions in the countryside. Do you remember others?

DEV: There was another that I remember very well, it was that of Mrs Flynn. I was hurling with Tom Mortell on the side

of what we used to call Mortell's Hill. When we were tired
we sat down. I had been warned not to sit on wet grass, so I sat
on the 'bos' [broad part] of the hurley and we were both
looking north-west when I saw this funeral winding around
from the house, across over the Railway Bridge at Howardstown. 'Twas very distinct to me as the hearse and the other cars
passed by. It set me thinking on death, on life, on the shortness
of life, and the hereafter and that set me wondering about the
world around me - whether it really existed or whether it was
a dream; and to satisfy myself, anyhow, I pinched Tom
Mortell who was beside me. The response I got left me in no
doubt as to the actuality of the world outside me. I
remembered that during the whole of my life. It may have
been the reason why on one occasion a professor of meta-
physics called me a crude realist. I wasn't, of course, a crude
realist, but I had no doubt as to the reality of the external
world!

*   *   *   .

DONNCHA: Do you remember the mission?
DEV: At a mission once there was a very funny thing. You
know, the old women would come along with their donkeys,
like my grandmother would, but this old lady used to come to
this mission in Rockhill alone, and there was a gate down
about one hundred yards from the church on the left-hand side
and 'twas convenient for tying her donkey while she went on
to the mission. So, this night when she came out she found that
the donkey was inside the gate. They had untackled him while
she was inside, put him inside the gate, pushed the shafts
through the gate and tackled him again. The poor woman was
wondering how he got through the gate. Some of the prime
boys said, 'That's a miracle for you!'

Next, I remember we were coming home from a mission.
My uncle was with my grandmother and myself. They were
racing the donkeys home after the mission. There was a bit of
a hill from the Schoolhouse Cross in Rockhill down to

Rourke's Cross. My uncle won the race the first night. So the others made up their minds that he wouldn't do that again on the second night. So the race went on the second night.

We were half-way between Schoolhouse Cross and Rourke's Cross, when off came the wheel of the car. Some prime boy had taken the linchpin. Curiously enough we weren't thrown headlong. There was a jolt when the axle came to the ground against an upward slope, but none of us fell out.

DONNCHA: It seems that entertainment was provided by yourselves in an *ad hoc* way rather than on an organised basis. Did you have house dances?

DEV: They had a big dance which they called a ball. The principal instrumentalist at the ball was a man named Flaherty who played the pipes - he was noted for playing particularly 'The Fox Chase'. Each person paid one shilling or something like that and they got refreshments during the night and they had a really good time. There were quite a number of people who were really good dancers. We had one famous dancer who was called Maurice the Dusht [Limerick pronunciation of dust!]. He used to dance on the road very often and in those days there was dust on the roads, and I have no doubt that it was from the amount of dust that was knocked up when he was dancing, perhaps a hornpipe, that he got his name.

DONNCHA: Did you ever learn to dance yourself, a Uachtaráin?

DEV: I can't say that I learned very well! My grandmother sent me to get some lessons in dancing. There was a dancing master who went from place to place and when he was in Bruree my grandmother told me that I should go down and get some lessons. I was taught the side-step, the jig and one or two of the set dances, but I'm afraid I didn't practise dancing at all.

*   *   *

DONNCHA: An raibh mórán Gaeilge le fáil i mBrú Rí, nuair a bhí tusa óg?

DEV: Bhí Gaeilge ag na sean-daoine go léir. Nuair a thagaidís le chéile is i nGaeilge a bhídís ag caint. Is minic a bhíos ag éisteacht leo agus ní rabhadar toilteanach Gaeilge a labhairt leis na daoine óga. Bhí fáth ann dar ndóigh. Ach thaitin an Ghaeilge liom-sa go maith. Is cuimhin liom ceist a chur ar mo sheanmháthair. D'iarr mé uirthi abairt Ghaeilge a thabhairt dom. Ní raibh sí toilteanach. Ansan, dúirt mé, 'How would you say in Irish, give me a chair?' Agus dúirt sí, 'Tabhair dom cathaoir', agus b'shin í an chéad abairt Ghaeilge a bhí agam. Ach, cé nach raibh an Ghaeilge á labhairt ag na daoine óga, bhí na logainmneacha agus a lán focail eile acu.

*   *   *

DONNCHA: Were politics talked of around your uncle's hearth? What are your first political recollections?

DEV: As far as my political recollections are concerned, my uncle used to read the paper for my grandmother and I was sleeping in the loft upstairs and I could hear whatever went on in the kitchen. So, my uncle used to read the news and I used to listen in, if I was awake.

My first recollection, I think, was the shootings in Mitchelstown and the horror expressed by my uncle and my grandmother at this terrible business. Then, after that, the time that William O'Brien escaped from Tullamore Jail - John Mandeville, I think, was with him at the time. Then Mandeville died later. These are my early memories.

There may have been an earlier one, I'm not sure. I was taken by my grandmother, 'twas on a Sunday, to a boycotting meeting of John Gubbins. Fr Sheehy, I think it was, who led the boycott. There were some tenants who were being evicted, or rents raised or something like that. The Fedamore Band had come into Bruree to play at the meeting. The drum attracted me because I had been given a present of a drum myself and I put a cord on it 'round my neck to try to beat it with sticks. This was a grand big drum and I could have given it a good hammer, without hurting my knuckles! The

Fedamore big drum is associated with my first political recollections. I do not know if it came before the Mitchelstown shootings or not.

When my grandmother took me to Bruree to the boycott meeting I was in petticoats and I had long hair — my grandmother was rather proud, if I might put it that way, of my hair. It was of a golden colour, I believe! She wanted me to keep on wearing it long. My uncle, on the other hand, had more regard for my feelings on the matter and he wanted to cut it off. On one occasion he did cut it off and my grandmother was very, very angry.

Later, of course, I used to hear about the Parnell Commission and I remember my uncle telling my grandmother, 'Pigott shot himself in Madrid yesterday morning.' It was evidently in the papers next day, so I wanted to know who Pigott was and so on.

Then the next thing about Parnell was when it was found that *The Times* were wrong and how pleased they were when the verdict went in favour of Parnell. Then, of course, I heard about the divorce afterwards and the sadness that was in our part of the country. My uncle would be typical of the feeling - very sad about the whole thing. Someone had suggested that Parnell should resign for a time and that was thought to be the commonest view. That's what they were hoping around our part of the country. They didn't, of course, realise the whole situation.

DONNCHA: Your uncle Pat was, obviously, a significant figure in your early life?

DEV: My uncle was elected a member of the Kilmallock District Council. He was also one of the very first to get into the land and labour organisation. I remember he went to Limerick Junction to a meeting establishing it there. William Field from Dublin, I knew him well later, was there.

DONNCHA: Was there a good national spirit around Bruree at that time?

DEV: Certainly. They were strongly nationalistic. No doubt about that.

DONNCHA: Now, you mentioned a priest, Fr Eugene Sheehy, who was prominent in land agitation. Would you like to tell me a little bit about him?

DEV: Well, he was one of the great Land League priests, very much on the side of the tenants. He was arrested by Clifford Lloyd and imprisoned in Kilmainham. He was there at the same time Parnell was there. He had a good reputation in the parish.

I remember him best, of course, from being an altar boy. I used to serve his Mass when he said it in Bruree. I often sat on the side of the altar and listened to his sermons. He spoke, in my opinion, very well. We had a special day, of course, on St Munchin's Day, which was the 2nd of January. That was a free day for us boys, anyway, and was, probably, a holiday for the whole parish. On that day, frequently, we had a preacher from outside. I remember one or two very eloquent sermons given by these preachers. I preferred, myself, to hear Fr Sheehy speak than anybody else. He spoke to us of the glories of Bruree. He told us how it had been the stronghold of Oileal Olum, the progenitor of the kings of Munster, both Eoghanacht and Dail gCais. He referred to the Raithíní, little forts on the bank of the river. He spoke of Cnoc Dotha and, of course, spoke of O'Donovan's Castle. Fr Sheehy made us feel that Bruree was not merely the head of the diocese but that it was the head of Munster, and, of course, through the Dail gCais the head of Ireland. For many of us, indeed, it seemed to be the centre of the universe!

*   *   *

DONNCHA: How ambitious were your Bruree relatives for your future?

DEV: I know that my grandmother had hoped that she might be able to apprentice me to be a carpenter. I would have liked that, of course, but fundamentally I think my desire was to become a priest. I'm not sure that I had any definite ideas about it however.

DONCHA: Was Ireland much in your thoughts at that time?

DEV: Well, of course, I had imbibed the sort of national feeling that was common around the country and was in my own home and, of course, dislike of the invader. My uncle had a big book on Irish history, the Abbé MacGeoghegan's *History of Ireland.* It was the book that he would read occasionally, but the book that I read from most was A. M. Sullivan's *The Story of Ireland.* It was the first history of Ireland that I really read. Of course I don't know to what extent the historians of today would stand by what's in it but it gave you a feeling for and a love of your country.

DONNCHA: Stories of your exploits in 1916 are still told in Bruree. Did you return home soon after the Rising?

DEV: I think the first time that I came to Bruree after 1916 was just before the Clare election. I went down there to address a meeting before I began the campaign. I remember we had a very big meeting in Bruree and I spoke there on a Friday because I went to Clare on a Saturday.

DONNCHA: Was this your first speech as a candidate for the election?

DEV: Well, in a sense it was. Everyone knew that I was to be a candidate, but I went to Bruree to speak to the people of Bruree first!

DONNCHA: You have visited Bruree many, many times over the years. Can you pinpoint any other occasion?

DEV: Yes. I went there to give a lecture some years ago in which I spoke about Fr Sheehy and how he used to speak on the particular spot from which I was speaking.

DONNCHA: Was this a long talk?

DEV: I'm afraid throughout my life I've had a very bad habit of talking too long! How my audiences remained listening for the length of time that I spoke, I often wonder!

Now, on one occasion, here in Dublin, I gave a talk on the Holy Land. I'd been to the Holy Land and I thought that these people to whom I was speaking would like to listen to it. This was an old men's home and it was coming on to ten o'clock at night and I think one of the old men wanted to get free. In any case, he had been asked to propose a vote of thanks. He began in this way: 'We have had a most exhaustive and, indeed, if I might add, a most exhausting lecture.' That reminded me that there must have been many people who are of the opinion that many of my talks have been if exhaustive, also exhausting!

* * *

DONNCHA: Do you often go back to Bruree now?

DEV: Not so very often. Now that I'm not able to see very well I'm not able to see the countryside. I go whenever I can. I always love to go there of course. Often I used to wish that I had my sight so that I might wander along by the brook again from Drumacummer right up to Trinity Well, where it starts in Dromin, and see some of the bushes that I thought must still be growing there and look into the water and see which minnows and so on were there and what birds would be nesting along in the bushes. But, of course, I can't do that. One of my regrets is that I can't see the whole countryside. I can imagine myself on the top of Knockdoha, over the village on the way to Rockhill, looking down north towards Tory Hill and looking east towards Kilmallock and west towards the mountains of West Limerick and on towards Kerry and then the Ballyhoura Hills to the south, seeing the whole countryside around. But I have to depend on imagination now. And I get annoyed because, of course, the sides of the road are covered with bushes that weren't there in my time. I'm sure they obscure the view. There should be some attempt to get these bushes cut down! In the old days they were cut down because in the wintertime the men on the farm who were sent out to clear up the drains and fix the hedges cut down the bushes half through and pulled them over on the side. That made a very fine fence and the view was not obscured in the way that it is now. The very tall bushes now are worse than the old walls.

DONNCHA: How close is Bruree to you today? Is it still important to you?

DEV: Oh, I think that loving one's immediate surroundings is

very natural and we naturally widen it as our horizon gets
wider. If you love your parish and your own little community
you'll widen it so as to embrace the nation as a whole. I'd like
to think that my love of Ireland originated in Bruree.

Biography

Eamon de Valera drew mocking criticism when he said,
'When I wanted to know what the Irish people thought, I
looked into my own heart.' But a wise Frenchman asked,
'Where else would he look?'

De Valera's public career spanned nearly six decades. He
was born in 1882, the same year as James Joyce, and after he
sprang into prominence with his defence of Boland's Mills in
the 1916 Rising, he remained in the public eye until he retired
from the Presidency of Ireland in 1973, fifty-seven years later.

The principal events of his life are well known: his birth in
New York of a Spanish father and an Irish mother; his return
to Ireland as a child to be reared by his grandmother at
Knockmore, near Bruree, in the county Limerick; his
becoming a teacher of mathematics; marriage to Sinéad
Flanagan, another teacher; involvement in the struggle for
independence and emergence as a national leader.

So far, the story follows a pattern common enough in the
lives of revolutionaries. But the signing of the Treaty with the
British Government in December 1921 and the tragedy of the
Civil War which followed, between supporters of the Treaty
and its opponents who clung fiercely to the ideal of an Irish
Republic, brought personal desolation to de Valera. He did
not rank as a military leader during the 'war of the brothers';
when the republicans gave up the struggle in May 1923 and
dumped their arms he had reached the nadir of his fortunes.
He was forty years of age.

Three years later he formed a new political party, Fianna
Fáil, and began the struggle to rehabilitate the republican

cause. With funds raised in the United States, he founded the *Irish Press* as a republican daily paper in September 1931, and his tenacity brought his party to power in February 1932. The years in the wilderness were over.

As leader of the Fianna Fáil party, he remained in power for sixteen years, a continuous period of democratic government unequalled in modern Europe. His most significant achievements were the enactment of a new Constitution in 1937 and the Anglo-Irish Agreement of 1938. The Constitution enshrined the removal of the last vestiges of imperial rule; the Agreement handed back the ports which the British had held under the Treaty of 1921 for use in time of war.

In World War II, his policy of neutrality came under unremitting pressure from Britain, Germany and the United States; had the ports remained in British possession, the policy of neutrality could not have been sustained. At home, the Irish Republican Army presented another threat which he met with the strongest measures.

He was out of office from 1948 to 1951, came back to power from 1951 to 1954 and lost office again until 1957. In that year, 1957, he led his party back to power with the largest majority he had ever won. It was an astonishing performance for a man in his seventy-fifth year; his vigour and endurance electrified the huge crowds who flocked to his great outdoor meetings.

Two years later he was elected President of Ireland, an office he held for fourteen years, retiring in June 1973 at the age of ninety. He died on 29 August 1975.

Eamon de Valera's vivid recollections of his childhood in rural Limerick, as recounted to Donncha O Dúlaing, show how close he remained to his roots.

Micheál macLiammóir

Mary Cannon, secretary to Micheál macLiammóir and Hilton Edwards welcomed me to the house. 'He is not so well today,' she said, 'but he will join you shortly.'

There was then, as there always was about Micheál macLiammóir, a touch of drama, of magic, as I waited for him.

It was a sombre day in January, a day for being indoors, a day, I thought, ideal for reminiscence, for the recollecting of things past. I waited - silent, nervous.

MacLiammóir entered with quiet theatricality.

'Dear boy, you are most welcome!'

The voice, the once great voice of our greatest actor, was quiet, tired, already reflective. Mary Cannon supervised the arrangements - seating, coffee. Small talk was undertaken, the fire was stoked up and macLiammóir sat back in his armchair. His eyes were sad and his mien was weary. There was an air of tiredness about him.

I was loathe to break his train of thought but it was time to urge Micheál macLiammóir towards the past. There was here a sense of occasion, a notion that something unique was in the wings. How right, how sadly right I was, for this was to be Micheál's last interview. It would not be too long before he would be at rest, a great shade among the great shades we were soon to talk of: Wilde, Chopin, the Countess [Markievicz], Shaw, Yeats, and all the others.

We went gently into the dim past as with voice and gesture he opened his heart to me and filled my mind with the riches of his life.

Micheál mac Liammóir.

MICHEÁL: 'The time has come the walrus said, To talk of other things . . .'

DONNCHA: Micheál, you were born a Corkman.

MICHEÁL: I was. [*On a rising Cork-like note!*]

DONNCHA: Where?

MICHEÁL: Blackrock.

DONNCHA: Do you have many memories of your Cork childhood?

MICHEÁL: Yes, very early childhood. We left when I was seven and that started my 'seven' racket - everything happened to me in sevens. We left Cork for London when I was seven. I came back from London to live in Dublin in 1917, I forget the date. My greatest friend in the world who is a cousin of mine called Máire O'Keeffe, on the O'Keeffe side of my mother's family, died on the 7th of January, 1929. On the 17th of June in 1927 I met Hilton Edwards. So, sevens are significant to me. A number of fate, good or bad, you know.

DONNCHA: You were a child of the theatre. Did that make life difficult for you as a boy?

MICHEÁL: Oh no - divine! It made it more lovely than ever. The one reason I thank God for our great poverty is because we all had to work. All my sisters had to go out and work instead of attending university and what not. They all had to be sales girls in shops, telephone girls in telephone exchanges.

My mother, one day after we'd gone to London, read an advertisement in, I think, *The Daily Mirror* about 'pretty, intelligent and talented children wanted. A professional engagement for a play by Miss Lelia Field for children entirely, no one over fourteen.' We all played in this play called *The Goldfish*. It was because we were so poor that I went on the stage.

DONNCHA: What did the rest of the family think of you?

MICHEÁL: Oh, delighted! They were very proud of me. They spoilt me I'm sure.

My family was curious. They had four daughters, all born within two years of each other. Then a gap of six years in which nothing happened and then I appeared to the delight of my father. A son, at last!

I have one lovely sister, the only one still alive, God bless her and keep her. Only she's not a bit happy. She'd be much happier dead. I never pity dead people. I pity the people they loved and left behind. I think dead people are very lucky, you know. But she is not happy at all. She's six years older than I am and she was my youngest sister.

DONNCHA: I suppose bereavement, being left behind, is one of the saddest things in life.

MICHEÁL: Don't you find that?

DONNCHA: I do, I do.

MICHEÁL: And two elderly women, my dear friends, both of them deeply unhappy and in 'homes' which does not suit them.

DONNCHA: I suppose, in a sense, that 'home' is a misnomer there.

MICHEÁL: Ah, nursing homes you know. You're just a number for a certain nurse.

It's all very dreary - life - I think.

*   *   *

DONNCHA: Let's look at people who have amused you during your life. Say, famous people?

MICHEÁL: [*Laughs*] Oh, I've known so many. Famous and amusing, famous and not so amusing, infamous and amusing. You could go on forever.

DONNCHA: You have written a book on Yeats. When did you first meet Yeats?

MICHEÁL: Oh, I will never forget it. His first remark to me was crushing. I had longed to meet him as my hero and as the only man who had influenced my life. People think that I am immensely influenced by Oscar Wilde. I'm not in the least! I'm a great admirer and I have a ghostly friendship - with the man I never met, naturally. Even I am not old enough to have remembered Wilde! He died the year I was born, I think. The year afterwards, perhaps, or the year before, I forget. I was born at the end of 1899, at the very end of it, October 25th

1899. I share a birthday, in everything but the year, with Picasso.

DONNCHA: We were talking about Yeats, about meeting him.

MICHEÁL: Oh, yes, Yeats. I'd longed to meet Yeats all my life and the first thing he said to me - extending a pearl-pale hand covered with jewels, all of mystical significance (I don't know whether I was supposed to shake it or kiss it, so I decided on the former action because I thought that if I kissed his ring, that he, being a Protestant, would be shocked) - the first thing he said was, 'You told Lady Gregory you had waited for fourteen years to meet me. You're exactly fourteen and a half minutes late!' He knocked me flat.

I said how sorry I was and that a rehearsal had kept me and so on. He then picked me up by saying, 'You are a magnificent actor!' So, what do you do with a man like that? He was a demon, but very fascinating.

DONNCHA: There seemed to be a tremendous quality of genius, but also a bizarre side to him, which, maybe, is quite inseparable from genius, at times.

MICHEÁL: He lacked humour terribly, I think. He may have had a grim sort of humour of his own, but nobody who could have fallen in love with Maude Gonne could have much of a sense of humour.

DONNCHA: Did you know Maude Gonne, too?

MICHEÁL: Indeed I did. Would you like me to go on?

DONNCHA: I would indeed.

MICHEÁL: [*Laughing*] Poor 'Maude Gonne mad' as she used to be known by the Dublin chiselers, 'Maude Gonne Mad and Mrs Desperate' - that was Mrs Despard, sister of Lord French.

DONNCHA: You have very happy memories of Howth?

MICHEÁL: Oh, very. I always regarded it quite falsely, as my home. It was the place I loved the best in Ireland when I came back in 1917 to live in Dublin for the first time in my life.

My only knowledge of Dublin was one visit to an uncle who had married a Dublin woman and lived on the North Circular Road, and another when I toured in *Peter Pan*. We were here for a week in 1913 during the strike, in which

Madame, the Countess Markievicz, was very prominent.
DONNCHA: Did you know her?
MICHEÁL: Quite well. I was rather fond of her except that she represented everything I loathed - gunshot and killing policemen and carrying on something cruel! There's a picture of her, I still have it, which she gave me of herself in Citizen Army uniform. She's leaning on a sort of plinth, with a hat of cock's feathers and a revolver in her hand, looking so crazy that you wouldn't have trusted her with a child's pea-shooter!
DONNCHA: They use an expression nowadays that's very popular - charisma. Did she have it?
MICHEÁL: Charisma, yes. Well, she had charisma. She had it more than Maude Gonne. She was absolutely sweet to me. She couldn't have been nicer. But she was so utterly devoid of humour it was rather difficult for me to get on with her.
DONNCHA: Pearse, of course, was gone when you came here.
MICHEÁL: Pearse was gone. Pearse was a sacred name. And I am convinced that he had two guilt complexes, one, that he was half English, like so many of our great leaders, and the other I won't mention now, but he had a thing on his conscience. He was a good Catholic, I think.
DONNCHA: Micheál, this business of being of mixed blood has been a great asset to the race.
MICHEÁL: Indeed, of course, as it has been to every race. [*There was a long pause and Micheál continued.*] Now, Italy . . . there's a country for you! What artists . . . think of Michelangelo . . . think of him for a second . . . think of Greece . . .
DONNCHA: When you think of Michelangelo which of his works do you like to dwell on?
MICHEÁL: The 'David', I think. Mind you his vision was very limited. It was practically limited to the male body, the male torso. His women are like men, with breasts on. His feeling for anything beyond the human body, the male human body, especially, was very primitive. You find his marvellous Adam lying on a non-existent hill - just a line for a hill, with this magnificent creature lying on it touching God's finger, and God, leaning out of rather indifferent clouds, touching

Adam with the tip of his finger.

DONNCHA: What does 'David' signify? What do you find in it?

MICHEÁL: David himself, God forgive me, means very little to me. But Michelangelo's 'David', it means a great deal to me. I suppose it is one of the most ravishing things that I've ever seen.

* * *

DONNCHA: Did you think much of growing old?

MICHEÁL: I never thought of old age, dear boy, never, never in my life. It never occurred to me. I presumed that it would come and I used to look at old people and pity them, but that was all. I never thought of it happening to me.

DONNCHA: How does it seem to you now?

MICHEÁL: To be old?

DONNCHA: Yes.

MICHEÁL: Bloody awful! That's the only thing that Maude Gonne ever said to me that I thoroughly agree with: 'Micheál dear, they talk about the beauty of old age. Don't believe a word of it. It's hell!' So it is. There's nothing nice about it. It took the genius of a Rembrandt to portray the beauty in old faces. But, in effect, in old age there is nothing but depression, sadness. I agree again with dear Oscar: 'Our limbs fail, our senses rot. We degenerate into hideous puppets, haunted by the memory of what we once were!'

DONNCHA: I suppose, in a sense, Micheál, memory is a two-edged sword.

MICHEÁL: Yes, how right you are. And yet when it begins to show signs of disappearing one is terrified. I am.

DONNCHA: Now we have drifted again into a sort of minor key.

MICHEÁL: A minor key. Ah well, why not?

* * *

Mac Liammóir in his later years.

DONNCHA: Why don't we talk about art, about painting, your own work?

MICHEÁL: My father had a most magnificent line in drawing and the least sense of business I've ever met - even in myself! He was no good at all! That's why we were so poor, because he didn't earn any money, practically.

DONNCHA: The artistic talent and a sense of business do not go together.

MICHEÁL: Oh, by God they don't! Very seldom do they go together. They did go together in Noel Coward. But then his own art was very, shall we say it, superficial.

DONNCHA: Was Coward as precocious and as clever as a child, as he was as a man?

MICHEÁL: Exactly. He has changed less than any human creature I've ever known. I knew him from the age of ten up until the year he died when he was in his late sixties. I was born on the 25th of October 1899, he was born on the 16th of December 1899 and one of his last remarks to me, wagging the old finger, was: 'Mickey darling, you and I were born the same year, but, in actual fact, you are six weeks and four days older than me, darling! Don't attempt to deny it!' That was the last thing he said to me. And the first thing he said to me -it was when we were children together, both of us ten years old, at a rehearsal of *The Goldfish* (in which I was supposed to be earning fifteen shillings a week and it was raised when I was put into the role of the Goldfish). We were all human children in the first act. I was Charlie and Noel was Jack, I think. In the second and third acts, for some unknown reason, we became either fish or jewels. I remember saying to him at that first childish meeting, 'What are you going to be when you grow up?' He replied: 'An actor of course! Why do you think I'm here?'

DONNCHA: He was the same from start to finish.

MICHEÁL: He never changed.

DONNCHA: His humour always seems to me to be very brittle, sharpish?

MICHEÁL: Brittle, Shakespearean. Shakespearean only in one

sense - Shakespeare, you know, never followed his own advice which he put in the mouth of Polonius: 'If brevity be the soul of wit . . .' Well, God knows, Noel was brief and very, very funny. When he saw the Queen of the 'Cannibal Islands' [Tonga] going to the coronation of the present Queen of England and he saw this magnificent coloured woman, presumably, sitting in a carriage with a very small man beside her, and someone asked, 'Who is he?' Noel said, 'Probably her lunch!'

DONNCHA: Let's talk about Oscar again. Oscar was a man who was very badly treated by life, wasn't he?

MICHEÁL: Oh, horribly. Mind you, he behaved very badly, foolishly. But, there you are, you see. He wasn't very wise. He was extraordinarily wise in some things and then amazingly stupid and careless in other things, as you see. That's why he came to grief.

DONNCHA: He was, obviously, a tremendous vehicle for your one-man show.

MICHEÁL: Well he meets you half-way, you see. Now the one-man show about Yeats is so difficult. It's all sheer beauty, sheer nobility and beauty of thought and nothing much else. Whereas Oscar has something marvellous to say about every moment of life, practically. Oh, yes, an amazing creature. This small - smallish - city, compared with London, Paris or New York, has produced great men in literature, especially when you think of Shaw and Wilde in the same generation. Utterly unalike.

DONNCHA: Did you ever meet Shaw?

MICHEÁL: Oh, I did. Two or three times.

DONNCHA: Did you like him?

MICHEÁL: No.

DONNCHA: Why not?

MICHEÁL: I thought he was a self-opinionated, egocentric old devil, who knew everybody's job better than they did. He knew more about religion than the priests. He knew more about medicine than the doctors and science than the scientists. He knew all about politics and the politicians. He knew more about everything, according to himself! The one talent he had not got really was the talent of the drama. He had no sense of humanity. He had a dazzling, brilliant brain about the abstract. But he was no dramatist. He wasn't interested in humanity, I think.

* * *

DONNCHA: You came back to Ireland, Micheál - wasn't it in 1917, you said?

MICHEÁL: Yes.

DONNCHA: And you've stayed all the years?

MICHEÁL: Yes, all these years.

DONNCHA: Does it mean more or less to you now, this Ireland you came back to?

MICHEÁL: More and less. What's broken my heart is the behaviour in the North.

DONNCHA: Do you think that your image of Caitlín Ní hUallacháin has changed?

MICHEÁL: Oh, yes. Yeats's image. The image of Ireland, Caitlín, was created by Yeats and died with him, really! Some of us see in Caitlín Ní hUallacháin this wonderful ideal, this fairy woman crowned with stars, this martyr, this heroine. As Yeats himself said, 'We have all bent low and low and kissed the quiet feet of Cathleen, the daughter of Houlihan.' But James Joyce has seen her as the old sow who eats her own farrow. One can see that angle too.

DONNCHA: Caitlín is a very complex woman.

MICHEÁL: She is like all countries. Countries are continually demanding the blood sacrifice of their children. Look at Yeats's play that practically created the image of Caitlín Ní hUallacháin in the Irish imagination, the play in which the preparation for a wedding is going on and the poor old woman comes to the door and it is Ireland herself. She goes down the street with him following her, to fight, to give his blood for her and the last line of the play is: ' "Did you see an old woman and you going down the road?" "I did not. But I saw a young girl and she had the walk of a queen." ' She'd got what she wanted, you see.

DONNCHA: In a way, I suppose, the whole recreation of nations, of national ideals, is a whole series of metamorphoses.

MICHEÁL: It is, really, isn't it? Shaw had the right idea about that. So good about abstract ideas. No good at putting them in concrete form. When he said that a healthy man is not conscious of his backbone and a healthy nation is not conscious of its nationality, but injure that backbone, warp it in some way and the man can think of nothing else, and injure the backbone of a nation and it is forever obsessed with a passion for putting that to rights again, until you can't get rid of it. That's Ireland's trouble. She can see nothing but ridding herself of the stranger.

DONNCHA: You were here during what's called the War of Independence. Did you ever meet people like Michael Collins?

MICHEÁL: I never met Michael Collins, I'm sorry to say, although I don't like his type. I mean, I don't like a great soldier figure, but I had an immense personal admiration for Michael Collins. He was a magnificent creature and that's why I was pro-Treaty, as they called it. Collins and Griffith were good enough for me. What they said, went.

DONNCHA: Did you meet de Valera?

MICHEÁL: Oh, I did. Politically I disliked him very much because he was one of the people who, with Mr Childers, came out against what the leaders of this country thought.

DONNCHA: How did he [Dev] seem to you when you got to know him personally?

MICHEÁL: Oh, charming. I liked him immensely, always did.

DONNCHA: It must have been a difficult time to be in the theatre?

MICHEÁL: Oh, 'twas desperate. We must pluck ourselves away from all this grief and think of something lovely . . .

* * *

DONNCHA Do you like New Years? Do you like the turn of the year?

MICHEÁL: No, I hate it. I dread it. I loathe it. I'm always afraid. I'm a coward at heart. I'm afraid of unhappiness. I'm afraid of more unhappiness coming.

DONNCHA: Do you feel that as the years wear on they seem to speed up?

MICHEÁL: No, on the contrary, I find that they slow down and creep by with feet of lead. That's what I feel. Even the time of day. I think: is it only nine o'clock? Good God! I thought it was midday at least, only nine, my God! And it goes on like this. What's the day of the week? Only Tuesday, my God, the weeks seem like years! Yes, I find it slow.

DONNCHA: Which poets do you like to think about? Would you like to say a verse or two?

MICHEÁL: One about the everlasting Caitlín Ní hUalacháin!
[*Then Micheál sat forward and began to recite.*]

The host is riding from Knocknarea
And over the grave of Clooth-na-Bare;
Caoilte tossing his burning hair,
And Niamh calling *Away, come away:*
Empty your heart of its mortal dream.
The winds awaken, the leaves whirl round,
Our cheeks are pale, our hair is unbound,
Our breasts are heaving, our eyes are agleam,
Our arms are waving, our lips are apart;
And if any gaze on our rushing band
We come between him and the deed of his hand,
We come between him and the hope of his heart.
The host is rushing 'twixt night and day,
And where is there hope or deed as fair?
Caoilte tossing his burning hair,
And Niamh calling *Away, come away.*

Then, one verse that he cut out in later years, which, I think, is
a pity, because it is lovely:

> *And brood no more where the fire burns bright*
> *Filling your heart with immortal dreams,*
> *For arms are waving and lips are agleam,*
> *Come away, come away to the dim twilight.*

I love that poem.

*   *   *

DONNCHA: Micheál, we are recording this conversation in the
dim twilight of a January evening at the turn of the year.
MICHEÁL: The dim twilight.
DONNCHA: You were talking about the voices saying come
away! Where do you think one goes at the end of this
existence?
MICHEÁL: Oh, Oh, Oh . . . you remind me of a conversation
with a very good friend of mine, Desmond Rushe of the
Independent. He said to me one day, quite simply, 'Do you
believe in God, Micheál?' I said, without any hesitation, 'Yes,
of course I do! 'Oh!' he said, 'I wish that I could say that with
such simplicity and such directness.' And we then went on
talking about God and an after life and so on. And I said, yes,
and that ultimately - ultimately I believed in the Christian idea
of heaven. It isn't only Christian, I know. Most religions
believe in heaven. And some of the poor misguided fools
believe in hell. However, I, personally, believe in heaven,
ultimately, but I don't think that we go straight there. I don't
think that any of us is ready for that, and I'm sure we're not
ready for hell and I don't think we ever will be. At the hands of
the God of love we are supposed to go through an infinity, an
eternity of ignoble torture, which we, with all our sins, would
not inflict, not for five minutes, let alone forever! Yet He's
supposed to do that to us, or allow it to be done to us as a
punishment for this or that, forever and ever and ever. The
idea is barbarous and, to me, ludicrous. No, I believe in a

system after death, but this is something very personal. I never say it to convert.

I believe in the theory of reincarnation, not necessarily on this earth but in some form in which I think the human spirit is born again into another body with all the sort of earthly experiences, the trials, the triumphs, unhappinesses, faults and everything else, what we all go through every day. It's the same system as rehearsing a play, if you like, in my profession, or as going to school in anybody's boyhood or girlhood. You go back and learn what you failed to learn before in order to pass a certain exam, and the exam, presumably, is for heaven.

DONNCHA: Are there people you would like to meet in another existence?

MICHEÁL: Yes, one especially of course. I'd like to meet Shakespeare, but I don't know would I ever. But of all the people in this history of the arts, and they're the only things that really interest me ultimately, I would like to meet Chopin, the composer. I'd like to meet him more than anyone, because to me he seems to talk in music of something I understand profoundly, or feel I do. And unlike Beethoven — a greater musician, I believe, but he is what Yeats would call 'so damnably predictable'. I always know what's coming next. Do you feel like that about listening to Beethoven?

DONNCHA: Perhaps. Why Chopin?

MICHEÁL: Because Chopin speaks a language that I feel. I understand. It's like listening to a man talking and you feel in sympathy with every word that he says and that you understand it, that you want to get nearer and nearer to it.

DONNCHA: What would you like to ask him?

MICHEÁL: I don't want to ask him anything! I just want to listen to him . . . to be told things.

DONNCHA: Which piece of his music to you like most?

MICHEÁL: Almost everything the damn man wrote. Almost everything. The only thing is that in my present, rather unhappy mood, frankly, he's a little too sad for me. As dear Oscar said, God rest him, 'He's marvellously romantic!' He says that in *Dorian Gray* somewhere, listening to a nocturne of

Chopin that Dorian is playing on the piano: 'He is so marvellously romantic, I wonder did Chopin ever write that?'

He [Chopin] was living with George Sand, as you know, somewhere in the Mediterranean, and what a dreadful woman she must have been. She used to call him 'mon petit malade', you know. But to me 'mon petit malade' speaks a language that I wish to God I knew and that I'd love to learn. I don't mean just to play him, I mean to understand all that seems to me to be said in his music.

*   *   *

DONNCHA: What is it makes you happiest nowadays?
MICHEÁL: [*Pauses and sighs.*]
DONNCHA: What is it that can throw a ray of sunshine through the window and lighten everything?
MICHEÁL: [*Another long, sad and reflective pause.*] Shall I be absolutely honest and answer that? Very little, except Hilton being well and happy.
DONNCHA: How is Hilton?
MICHEÁL: He's not well at the moment.
DONNCHA: It's been a great and marvellous partnership, hasn't it?
MICHEÁL: Oh, wonderful.

Biography

Member of the Irish Academy of Letters and of the French Legion of Honour, Freeman of the City of Dublin, Doctor of Laws of the University of Dublin, actor, painter, dramatist, stage designer, writer of fairy stories for children and of autobiographies, linguist, diarist, this was Micheál macLiammóir.

He called the second of his one-man shows 'I Must Be Talking To My Friends'. One feels on reading his conversa-

Mac Liammóir with his lifelong partner, Hilton Edwards.

tion with Donncha O Dúlaing that talking to his friends was one of his great pleasures.

After early childhood in Cork, where he was born in 1899, and a couple of years as a child actor in London, he spent several years in Spain and determined to be a painter. He studied in London at the Slade School, held exhibitions of his paintings in Dublin and then made a Grand Tour of Europe, wandering around for several years studying painting and languages in Germany, Italy, Switzerland and France. Then in 1927 he came home to Ireland for good, and formed his enduring partnership with Hilton Edwards, then a young English actor and opera singer.

1928 was a golden year in Irish theatre, an 'Annus Mirabilis'. On 27 August, Taibhdhearc na Gaillimhe opened its doors with a performance of macLiammóir's play, *Diarmuid agus Gráinne,* with the author playing the lead. He also designed and painted the set. Lady Gregory was in the audience. And on 19 October, the Dublin Gate Theatre Studio, founded by macLiammóir and Edwards, presented their first production in the 102-seater Peacock Theatre. It was Ibsen's *Peer Gynt,* to music by Grieg.

The settings were by macLiammóir. The stage was described by a critic as little bigger than an Edwardian dining table but the production electrified the audience.

The company moved to the present Gate Theatre in 1930, and brought to Dublin most of the major European plays of the time. Many notable Irish plays had their first production there. The partnership brought a great sense of style and a demanding professionalism to each production. They made many successful tours abroad, visiting Egypt, Greece, Malta and the United States. MacLiammóir's own best performances were in Shakespeare, especially as Hamlet. In 1952 he played that part at the Theatre Festival in Elsinore, Denmark, and received the Kronberg Gold Medal for his performance.

His creative output was prodigious. He wrote ten plays, three one-man shows and nine books on the theatre and his life in it, three of these in Irish. His faithfulness to the language never faltered; he kept up his command of it by writing his diary in Irish every night. His ideal was an Ireland Gaelic and European rather than Anglo-American. In 1960 the Irish Academy of Letters presented him with the Lady Gregory Medal for his contribution as a writer to the cultural life of the country. Previous recipients included W.B. Yeats and G.B. Shaw.

For Micheál macLiammóir, real life was in the theatre: 'The banquet of life begins for us when the half-hour is called . . . then, curtain up. All else is kitchen work.' His last call came for him on 6 March 1978.

Séamus Murphy

When Daniel Corkery died, Séamus Murphy joined me in the Cork studios to pay tribute to him. Séamus was not at his best in a radio studio and, to relax him I suppose, I asked if I could get him anything. His reply surprised me, 'I'd like a pint!' It was the only time before or since that I brought a pint into a studio.

When we concluded the tribute, Séamus rather tentatively suggested that I might like to come out to meet him on his own ground. I did. I remember it very clearly now, a cold sunny day in September 1973 when I visited Séamus Murphy in his own studio in Blackpool.

Inevitably, the conversation began with talk of his days in the national school in St Patrick's in Cork, where his idol, his mentor, O'Connor's mentor and O Faoláin's mentor, Daniel Corkery, was teaching.

<hr />

 SÉAMUS: He was teaching there and we couldn't but get involved with him, because he had an approach and a method which was very unusual and not shared by the other teachers in the estab-lishment. One of the things he did for everybody was to teach them how to draw. Despite the fact that there was only half an hour a week on the curriculum for it

Séamus Murphy.

[drawing], he gave us lessons and encouraged us to look at things, see things, use our eyes. In that way he woke up a whole lot of dormant things within us.

DONNCHA: He taught you to see. How?

SÉAMUS: He taught us to always be observing. He'd meet you and he'd say, 'Tell me now, on your way down to school this morning did you notice anything peculiar, anything happen, was there any event that struck you?' And of course you'd never see anything, but after a while when he'd keep on with this, you'd say, 'Well, there were two cars passed up.' And from cars he'd get to people. In that way he'd tell you: 'Always use your eyes. There's always something happening. There's always change.'

DONNCHA: Was this important to you?

SÉAMUS: Oh, very important to me because of curiosity. But – funny, you know – someone has to direct you to do a thing like that. You don't do it normally. At least, I wasn't doing it normally. But then, of course, you notice. You'd notice the skies. He was always telling us about the wonderful world of skies that we never look at. And we don't!

DONNCHA: Was Frank O'Connor in St Patrick's around your time?

SÉAMUS: No – well I suppose he would. He was my neighbour and lived within fifty yards of me. I remember him going to school, but we weren't in school at the same time, because he left at fifth book [fifth class] and went to the North Monastery. I didn't. I remained at St Patrick's and finished there. But I knew him in the neighbourhood of course, very well.

*   *   *

DONNCHA: Where did you go after St Patrick's, Séamus?

SÉAMUS: I went to work straight out of school. Corkery had sent us to the School of Art, a few of us, and a monument firm came in looking for a likely apprentice to stonecarving. So I was chosen and did a year to see if I'd like it and it worked out alright. I loved it. I continued then. I did a seven-year apprenticeship and then was a fully-fledged stonecarver. I went to the School of Art in the evenings and continued with the modelling.

DONNCHA: What was the money like at the time?

SÉAMUS: Well there was no money for the first year and I got half-a-crown for the second year. I got five shillings a week for the third year.

DONNCHA: You needed to have a taste for it, Séamus! Can you remember the first things that you modelled?

SÉAMUS: Well, I can remember the first thing that I carved - a tulip. But I don't remember the first thing I modelled. You were just given a plaster cast, usually some sort of architectural detail and you copied it. I can't remember the first thing, but I do remember the carving of the tulip because I carved it from an actual tulip and my terror was that I wouldn't have it finished by the time the tulip died!

*　　*　　*

DONNCHA: Looking around us in your studio we see a fair slice of Irish history, busts of many well-known people.

SÉAMUS: There are.

DONNCHA: When you look at a person to do a bust do you see a certain image which you pick on for a start?

SÉAMUS: Well, it's difficult to explain. I look and I get slowly involved, slowly by conversation and by talking and, eventually, there is some sort of mood established.

Sometimes it works and sometimes it doesn't. It can be very easy and it can be very difficult. There seems to be no sort of fixed way to go about it. I think 'tis communication. It takes two people to make a work of art. The sitter is just as important as the person doing it in so far as you will always get something from the sitter. If you don't, the work is stultified and boring. But, if there is some sort of contact, well, it enriches the work and it makes it interesting to you and I think, on the whole, that the thing flows better.

DONNCHA: Behind me here I see your bust of the Tailor, the

famous Tailor [of the book *The Tailor and Ansty,* by Eric Cross]. What was the Tailor like?

SÉAMUS: Well, the Tailor was the most wonderful person I ever met. I have never met anybody like him. He was an extraordinary, intelligent man and he was a man that knew the name of every wild flower in his neighbourhood and he knew everybody who passed up and down the road and he knew the skies and he knew the hedgerows, he knew everything. He was always pointing things out to you, noting them - animals, everything. The Tailor never had a dull moment.

DONNCHA: And you have a bust of Eric Cross who was almost his creator, if you like, alongside him.

SÉAMUS: Well, Eric knew the Tailor very well, of course. He met him for the first time I think around 1926.

DONNCHA: You knew Ansty as well?

SÉAMUS: Well, I did. They were a wonderful pair. One complemented the other. They were wonderful.

DONNCHA: A great humanity shines out through the Tailor's face.

SÉAMUS: Well, he was, he really was a humanist. He was a great person and a great storyteller.

DONNCHA: His end was sad, wasn't it?

SÉAMUS: Well, he was eighty-five. What happened to him over the book was sad. It should never have happened. However, he recovered from that and the neighbours came back to him.

DONNCHA: Oh! Did they?

SÉAMUS: Oh, yes, they all came back to him, eventually. They couldn't but! They saw that 'twas they who had committed sin not him when they broke in his windows and tried to keep people out of his house as a result of his book. But he recovered from that alright and we erected a nice stone to him in Gougane.

*   *   *

DONNCHA: Let's look around again at your studio. To the left here I see Tom Barry. Tom sat for you, did he?

SÉAMUS: He did, yes. He came most mornings and we got on very well. He was a very patient, a very good sitter. A most interesting man - I don't have to tell you that.

DONNCHA: You don't! What were you trying to capture in his face, Séamus?

SÉAMUS: I couldn't tell you really. I don't know. I just tried to see him with what they call artistic detachment, whatever that is. [*Here Séamus laughed.*] I got some side of him anyway.

DONNCHA: Yours is a very lonely craft in a sense isn't it? Here you are surrounded by the past and the present, all silent.

SÉAMUS: All silent! That's a great way to have them. [*Séamus was looking around and smiling at all the 'heads'.*] If an argument started here I'm afraid — well!

DONNCHA: yes, I can imagine Dev and the Tailor and Tom Barry and Seán Ó Riada involved.

SÉAMUS: Yes, and Máirtín Ó Cadhain and John Montague, and how many more of them?

DONNCHA: Seán Lemass and Maurice Walsh. And Michael Collins and the Countess [Markievicz].

[*There was much chuckling and laughing.*]

Yes, we'd certainly have some afternoon's entertainment if they all got going.

SÉAMUS: Well, there would be disagreement at various levels anyhow.

DONNCHA: Can you say which of your works has pleased you most?

SÉAMUS: It isn't possible because you'd say, I loved doing this and I loved doing that, but the point is I loved doing them all. Naturally enough some works cannot be as rewarding as others. I certainly enjoyed doing Tom because he is such a wonderful person and he has such a clear-cut concise mind.

* * *

DONNCHA: Is there something special about stone? Has it

In the studio at Blackpool with the 'heads'.

special meaning for you?

SÉAMUS: It has. You have to come to terms with it like you do with any other medium. It can be a very unyielding material, but if you get to know it and get to understand it you really get to love it, like you would timber, or any other material. And, you don't want to be able to master it by any means, because if you start mastering the thing the interest in it is lost. It is much better if it remains a challenging thing to you all the time.

DONNCHA: Always opaque?

SÉAMUS: Yes, and resisting you too. I'd prefer Irish limestone to anything, especially the Carlow stone, or Ballinasloe. Most of the limestone is good.

DONNCHA: Would you say, Séamus, that your style and technique have changed much over the years?

SÉAMUS: They have. But what I'm doing now is completely out of date compared with what's happening elsewhere. This is the last, really, of the old classical thing and nobody wants to model like that any more. They have gone on to other sorts of extensions which give them more scope. Everything now is abstract. What we would refer to as 'reality' doesn't enter in anymore. It must be contrived or lightened, and then you give it a fancy title.

DONNCHA: Séamus - perhaps to remain 'abstract' - what is reality to you in your own work?

SÉAMUS: Oh, that's a hard one. Well, in the case of a portrait, I expect to get something, always, from the sitter. If I don't, the work is arid. If there is communication between you and the sitter there is then an effort to reflect that, and, I think, you invariably do. You hear a person, you get to understand the personality, at least you think you do. That gives great satisfaction. The work improves. It's like technique. The more communication there is between you and the sitter, the better the work flows. There is no doubt at all about that because you are working in unison with somebody that you have an affinity with. Naturally what will evolve will be of some value.

DONNCHA: Who influenced you most? Corkery no doubt was

very important, but which craftsmen?

SÉAMUS: Well, mostly they were stone-carvers, mostly based in Dublin, but they were always travelling around. They came out of a very good tradition. They had been moving around, like their fathers before them, doing all the public buildings, including the years of the eighteenth century when Dublin was a great capital. It still is, but then it was one of the best cities in Europe. Many were trained by Italian craftsmen, plasterers, stone-carvers and figure-carvers who came over to embellish the eighteenth-century city houses and stayed and worked throughout the country. They went to England too and did the same thing there. They left a great residue of good craftsmanship after them which we had, one could say, right up to 1935. Now it has disappeared. There are no stone-carvers left. About four in Dublin, I'm about the only one here, and around the rest of the country it's gone. There's no need for it anymore with aluminium and glass. This new style hasn't found its own embellishment yet.

DONNCHA: Séamus, we were talking there about the stone-cutters. Can we talk about the stone-masons? Is that the same thing?

SÉAMUS: Well, it's the same thing. In country parlance 'tis the same, a stone-cutter and a stone-mason. To me, they're very much the same. They refer to stone-cutters in Dublin as masons, but in the country if you refer to a mason you are referring to what a stone-cutter in the city would refer to as a waller.

DONNCHA: A waller?

SÉAMUS: Yes, a waller, a man who builds rubble walls and stone walls and points them and puts them up. Now that's a stone-mason too. Now we've got to the stage of blockies. They are the fellows who put up concrete blocks and you have brickies who put up bricks. These are all split sections. They are all far removed from the stone-cutter. You have to make a distinction. The stone-mason in the country would be a mason who lays rubble stone walls and will set stone piers and will set cut stone. In the city, the man who cuts the stuff, joints it,

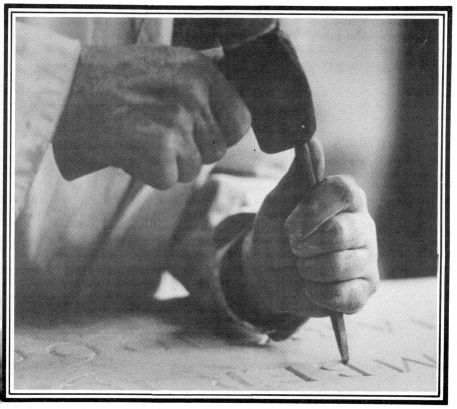

Séamus Murphy was famous for his superb lettering.

makes the beds - he is the stone-cutter.

DONNCHA: The masons were very much a breed in themselves.

SÉAMUS: They were. They were a closed trade from the guild times. You couldn't become a mason or a stone-cutter unless your father was one. Well I got in the back door because I didn't become a mason, I became a carver and the carvers were always distinct. They could only do foliage-carving, figure-carving and general decorative work. They weren't allowed to do the ordinary straightforward dressing of the stone.

DONNCHA: Didn't the masons have certain words of their own, a *patois* or a dialect?

SÉAMUS: They had - a jargon, the Béarlagar. 'Twas called Béarlagar na Saor. It's a secret language which came out in the guild period. They had quite a lot of them, just as the tinkers had the Shelta. There was another language also, the Béarlagar Shelta.

DONNCHA: Did you pick up any of the Béarlagar?

SÉAMUS: An odd word here and there. 'Twas gone, practically gone.

* * *

DONNCHA: Séamus, you were saying that you and the four or five others around are almost the end of a particular style or craft. How does this strike you?

SÉAMUS: Well, it's inevitable. The coachbuilders are gone. The blacksmiths are gone, they're replaced by garages. It's inevitable, Donncha.

DONNCHA: There's a very mechanistic life ahead of us.

SÉAMUS: There is. But it will always have its wonders too because there will be people trying to do something else with it. People will always try to change things. Sheer boredom makes them do it. They will try to alter things and if you don't do that you don't live at all. You are just repeating what had been done before. Every man wants to put his own stamp on something.

DONNCHA: Do you feel that you have done this?

SÉAMUS: I tried.

DONNCHA: You have commemorated everyone in sight in Ireland. How would you like to be commemorated?

SÉAMUS: [*Laughing*] I don't know. I don't think I have any interest in being commemorated, really.

DONNCHA: What do you think would be Daniel Corkery's reaction to your work if he were to come back to see it?

SÉAMUS: Oh, he'd be very pleased about it! Any endeavour would satisfy Corkery. He was dead set against the master-piece, the cult of the masterpiece which he said ruined all good writing and all good art. The important thing is to produce good work and when you get bored with the good work, you might then produce masterpieces. If you don't produce the good work, you cannot produce the masterpiece.

Biography

Séamus Murphy, sculptor and stone-carver said, 'If you wish to express yourself through an art form, you must have complete knowledge of one craft.' His own apprenticeship to his craft lasted seven years and he emerged a fully-fledged stone-carver.

In 1932, when he was twenty-four, he won a Gibson Bequest scholarship which took him to Paris for a year. He studied at the Academie Collo Rossi and with Andrew O'Connor, the Irish-American sculptor whom he much admired. The great boulevards had a special attraction for him. He walked around the city, examining the stone carvings on the buildings and studying the designs. At that time the student population of Montparnasse alone was about thirty thousand. Séamus revelled in the activity and life of the artists' quarter, feeling a sense of liberation and exhilaration in the company of those young men and women. The inhibitions fed by an upbringing in the Ireland of the early decades of this century could not withstand that onslaught. For the first time in his life he was able to model from life; nude models were not then allowed in the Cork School of Art.

When he returned to Cork in 1933, he held an exhibition and opened a studio. Times were hard and he got little to do until the Imperial War Graves Commission began erecting headstones for Irish soldiers who fell in World War I. Alfred O'Rahilly, then Registrar of University College Cork, commissioned him to execute a statue of St Finbarr to replace one of Queen Victoria. In 1936, the builders in Cork were out on strike for nine months and the stone-carvers were idle along with the carpenters and bricklayers. Séamus struggled on and gradually things improved. In 1944, William Dwyer, founder of Sunbeam Wolsey in Cork and one of the richest men in the south, commissioned him to design the Church of the Annunciation in Blackpool, as a memorial to Dwyer's daughter Maeve, and paid him a salary while he worked on it. Less successful was the bust of himself that Dwyer also commissioned. He did not like it and asked Séamus to scoop out the top so that he could use it as a bird-bath in his garden.

Headstones carved by Séamus Murphy can be seen in cemeteries all over the country. The simplicity and precision of the lettering and the austerity of the designs mark them unmistakably as his work. A fine example is the commemorative stone over the grave of his friend Seán O Riada in St Gobnait's cemetery in Cúil Aodha.

To Séamus Murphy, the traditional stone-cutters of his time were in direct line from the medieval craftsmen who built the great Gothic cathedrals of Europe. He tells the story of these men in his autobiographical *Stone Mad*, published in 1950. The work was hard, the craftsmen in a monumental stone-mason's workshop were known collectively as 'the Dust', and as a survival from the days of their medieval Guild, they got a pint of beer every morning at eleven o'clock. After a funeral, they walked about an art gallery, examining the headstones and monuments, and talking about the 'stonies' who carved them.

Stone Mad records a whole world of traditional skill and lore that is now gone, probably for ever. Difficulties were a challenge to their resourcefulness. When 'the Gobán' (they all had nicknames) found himself out on a job without a spirit level, he called for a basin of water, and gauged the level of the work by the tilt of the water in the basin. Another 'stonie', Paddy Brasswings, carving a cross for a country publican, put all kinds of foliage in it and then asked his master should he put a little dogrose in the corner. 'Don't, for God's sake,' said his master. 'You have every weed, briar and shrub in the country in it already.'

As his reputation grew, Séamus was commissioned to execute portrait busts of many famous people. In the entrance to Aras an Uachtaráin are placed bronze busts by him of all the Presidents from Douglas Hyde to Cearbhall O Dálaigh. His other commissions included heads of Sean Lemass, the 'Pope' O'Mahony, Archbishop McQuaid, Máirtín O Cadhain Michael Collins, Seán O Riada, Frank O'Connor and General Tom Barry. He was appointed Professor of Sculpture in the Royal Hibernian Academy in 1964 and in 1969 the National University of Ireland conferred the honorary degree of Doctor of Laws on him.

Séamus Murphy died suddenly on 2 October 1975 at his home at Wellesley Terrace, Wellington Road, Cork. He is survived by his widow, Maighréad, daughter of another Cork sculptor Joseph Higgins, two daughters, Bibhinn and Orla and a son, Colm.

Julia Grenan

Síghle Bean Uí Dhonnchadha is one of the most extraordinary women in Dublin. A veteran of the War of Independence and a lifelong republican, she was my guide and mentor in my various efforts to meet the lively and cheerful survivors of Cumann na mBan and the Citizen Army women who sometimes met at her Donnybrook home.

On one particular night she invited me to a 'little tea party to meet a few friends.' I arrived, bearing as always my tape-recorder. The 'few friends' present comprised as formidable a group of elderly ladies as I had ever met. They sat primly composed, waiting politely as I fumbled with tapes and nerves while Síghle and her daughter served tea.

The introductions were helpful. 'This is Julia Grenan, one of the last women in the GPO in Easter Week. And over here is Phyllis Bean Uí Cheallaigh who was also out in 1916. This is Margaret Skinnider who fought with the Countess in the Green and over here is Eily O'Hanrahan-O'Reilly, sister of Micheál O hAnnracháin who was executed in 1916 and, lest I forget, I'd like you to meet, too, Nora Connolly-O'Brien, daughter of James Connolly.'

I was quite stunned. Where or with whom could I begin? I looked around and no one spoke. So, as she was nearest, I turned to Julia Grenan, and Julia, a frail little wisp of a woman, smiled and asked, 'What do you want to know?' The others all sat forward in their seats and what followed was an almost communal interview as, with nods and smiles and

Julia Grenan (right) and her lifelong friend Elizabeth O'Farrell who brought the message of surrender from Pearse to General Lowe.

gentle expressions of approbation, these marvellous women of the Revolution remembered the greatest days of their lives.

———————

JULIA: It was Máire Peroltz who told me the Rising was definitely on. On Saturday night Roddy Connolly came and he mobilised the two of us for Liberty Hall, although we were Cumann na mBan. However Connolly sent for us and we went over and he said that he was going to attach us to the Citizen Army. We saw no objection to this because the Volunteers weren't taking any notice of us, didn't care whether we were there or not.

On Monday morning, about 3.00 a.m., Máire Peroltz and Charlie Power came to the house with the dispatches and I got three dispatches. I was to go to Dundalk and to Carrick-macross and my friend was to go to Athenry. The dispatches I had were for Patrick Hughes.

I went to Mass at 7.30 a.m. on Easter Monday morning. My friend and I parted at the corner of Earl Street. I went down Talbot Street to get the Northern train and she went up to the Broadstone. When I got into the train who also got in but a group of young girls in holiday attire, and one of them was Nora Connolly. I guessed what her business was. I got out at Dundalk. Nora Connolly was leaning out of a window. I went over to her and said, 'I hope that the next time we meet, it will be in a free Ireland.'

*   *   *

Later, I went on messages in Dublin to find out what was happening and report to the GPO. I went down to the Mendicity but I had to come back with no news at all and Connolly told me that I was the twentieth or the twenty-second he'd sent down to get news and there was still none.

Pearse didn't appear much at all, but Connolly sent me down to the Four Courts and when I went down to the Four Courts there was a woman there. I had a dispatch for Frank Fahy, but I gave it to Joe McGuinness because he was at the railings. There was a woman there and she was giving out dog's abuse about The O'Rahilly. She called the poor man everything and anything and she said that her son was in the Four Courts fighting but O'Rahilly wouldn't come out to fight. I needn't tell you, I put her right. 'And,' says she, 'are you saying he's up in the Post Office?' 'Oh,' I said, 'I know The O'Rahilly well. He's up in the Post Office.' 'I must tell me son,' says she. 'I must tell me son.' I hope she did.

When I came back from the Four Courts in the course of the day I met The O'Rahilly and I told him my story. 'Now, are you sure,' he asked, 'that you told that woman that you saw me and that you knew me?' 'I did, I did,' says I. 'Well,' he said, 'you have done me a great service. I'm very grateful to you and when we're in occupation here for a week we'll have a ball and I'll dance a minuet with you.' God help him! We didn't last the week at all.

Later that evening Connolly came to me and he said to me, 'Well,' he said, 'they obeyed your orders!' 'What orders?' said I. 'The ones,' he said, 'that you gave them in the Four Courts.' 'I didn't give any orders,' says I. 'Didn't you carry a dispatch telling them to blow up the Linen Hall!' he said.

* * *

One day Pearse called me and he said, 'I want you to do a very dangerous mission. This is a letter to the British and you'll have to go to the British lines with it. I don't mind if you refuse.' I said, 'Well, I came to do what I'm asked to do and I'm doing that!' 'So,' he said, 'I'll get the letter for you and you can refuse if you like.' It was to the Commander of the British Forces in Ireland, and in it Pearse said that the British had burned down a Red Cross unit we had on the far side of

O'Connell Street, on Clery's side. If this happened again, he had hostages and something would happen. So I said to him, 'Well now, may I bring my friend with me, because it would be better for two together than one on her own to be out on the street.' 'Oh, certainly,' he said.

At any rate we started off and outside the GPO we met Seán O'Mahony and his little friend, Murray, and I asked him how near we were to the British lines and he said Dorset Street and the two of us headed up Dorset Street and there wasn't a sight of a British soldier there.

I forgot to tell you that earlier in the week the two of us, along with a little girl, went from the Post Office with ammunition and Connolly gave us money and he said, 'Buy us food!' We had a terrible time getting across Dame Street. The British were lined up on both sides of the street and this little girl, Mary McLoughlin - she was very small, she was only about fourteen you know - I said to her, 'You run across the road there and if they stop you you're looking for your brother!' She got safely over and we got up to the College of Surgeons. We bought cheese. And there was a shop in York Street - she [the shopkeeper] was a member of the Clan - and I asked her for two dozen loaves and she asked me would she send them down: 'You needn't bother,' says she, 'I'll send them down!' I was delighted with that. Then the little McLoughlin one bought stuff too and she had one penny left. Connolly made her keep the penny!

I don't remember ever getting a bit to eat in the GPO and I don't ever remember sleeping! That's as true as I'm here! I think I lived without eating!

* * *

But, at any rate, one day Connolly went out. I didn't know that he had gone out until he was wounded and he told us that he went out to place three men in outposts in Middle Abbey Street. One of them was Seán Milroy and the other was Bill Ross who was a tailor. I mustn't have known the third man, for

I don't remember his name. Connolly told us, 'When I was coming back, I just turned down the lane and then stepped back to see if they were in their positions and that was when I was wounded.' He was knocked out and he said that the pain was intense.

He said, 'When I was lying there in the lane I thought of how often you two went up and down there and nothing ever happened yez!' And he told how he had to crawl on his hands and knees from Abbey Street up to Princes Street and when he got there he called for help. No one, of course, could hear him and he was very bad. Jim Ryan was the doctor there and helped him. There were also British officers there, some of them medicals, and they performed an operation on him.

* * *

DONNCHA: Can you remember what the atmosphere was like in the GPO as Easter Week drew to a close?
JULIA: It was very sad. Of course it was lovely when Pearse would read out the little statements. I nearly fainted with joy and delight when he said, 'We have redeemed Dublin! We have wiped out the stain of Emmet!' I nearly went down through the ground with joy! What a beautiful voice he had, what a beautiful voice!

But then he called Cumann na mBan and he told them that he would like them to leave. Of course they protested strongly. 'Now,' he said, 'at first that was a request. Now it is an order!' 'And,' he said, 'I'm very grateful, and, of course, Ireland is very grateful for the work you have done!' Fortunately, Winnie Carney, Elizabeth O'Farrell and myself were selected to go with the men to Moore Street.
DONNCHA: How was the GPO evacuated?
JULIA: The O'Rahilly was in charge of two rows of men, and Seán McDermott - oh, Seán McDermott was roaring, roaring like a lion at them. He was indeed!
DONNCHA: What was he saying to them?
JULIA: We had to run from the Post Office, to zigzag across to

Pearse surrenders

the lane. And we got across and some of the lads went, ran into houses in Henry Place, and Joe Plunkett said, 'Come out, ye cowardly curs!' They were terrified you know, terrified.

At any rate, we got into the house on the corner of Moore Street and Connolly was there, lying on a stretcher, and Seán McLoughlin was kneeling alongside him on one knee. And my friend went over to Connolly and she said to him, 'How are you now?' 'Bad,' he said. 'The soldier who shot me did a good day's work for the British Parliament!' He was getting worse and worse. We were there for the night.

I read [later] that it was Pearse who saw three men being shot dead while carrying white flags, and that he decided to surrender. The surrender was called.

We came out of the house. Seán McLoughlin was in charge. Now James Connolly gave Seán McLoughlin his rank and that's denied. Seán knelt at his side and when he stood up he said, 'James Connolly has given me his command.' That is denied, but that's the truth. It really happened.

At any rate we came out and on the edge of the path at Henry Place, there was a Volunteer and the Volunteer had his hands outstretched and when I saw him like that, I thought of the poor old croppy stretched out on the mountain-side. [*Here Miss Grenan wept.*] God help him, he was turned towards the wall. This poor fellow, he certainly looked very noble he did, very noble-looking.

So, we went up O'Connell Street then and the British soldiers were at the corner of Henry Street and they swinging their revolvers cursing us into the ground and out of it. However we went up and we were put sitting and lying on the grass plot. We were with the Headquarters crowd.

When we were giving our names the British said to Seán MacDiarmada, 'I see you have cripples in your army!' 'Now,' MacDiarmada said, 'You have your place, sir,' and his eyes used to sparkle with fire. 'I have mine and you had better mind your place, sir.' I was delighted.

A few spaces from me, up in Earl Street, there were Volunteers and didn't one of them [British Soldiers] say to one of the men in ordinary clothes, 'What are you doing here? Aren't you from my regiment?' And he said, 'I was arrested. The rebels arrested me.' 'Where's your uniform?' 'They stripped me of it,' he said. He called some soldiers and that young man, I didn't get his name, lived in Liverpool in a street called Buckingham Street . . . and he was like a young Irishman. [*Miss Grenan wept and was unable to continue.*]

Biography

Julia Grenan, a Dublin woman, was one of the members of Cumann na mBan, who, like Leslie Price (Leslie Bean de Barra), was out in the Rising of Easter Week, 1916. These young women sallied out from the GPO and the other buildings occupied by Volunteers into a city swarming with British troops and carried dispatches from post to post. They seemed to bear charmed lives.

By command of Pádraig Pearse, all the Cumann na mBan members in the GPO left the shattered building on the Thursday afternoon of that week, save for Julia Grenan, Elizabeth O'Farrell and Winifred Carney. It was Elizabeth O'Farrell who was asked by Pearse to take his message of surrender to the Commander of the British forces, Brigadier-General Lowe.

After the surrender, Julia Grenan was arrested and spent the Saturday night, 29 April, on the plot of grass in front of the Rotunda Hospital. The area was uncomfortably crowded with four hundred prisoners in a space that could accommodate only less than half that number, and the night was very cold. Afterwards, she was confined in Kilmainham Jail and heard volleys of rifle-fire on four mornings, as the leaders were being executed by firing squad. With a number of other Cumann na mBan members, she was released on 9 May 1916.

Julia Grenan worked as a furrier in a large Dublin store. In later years she was employed in the Hospitals Trust Office in

Ballsbridge. She lived quietly in Mount Street with her comrade of Easter Week and lifelong friend, Elizabeth O'Farrell. Their allegiance to the republican ideal never wavered. They collected money regularly for republican prisoners and their families and devoted themselves to helping them in every way. As long as they were able to, the two friends attended every republican function in Dublin.

Julia Grenan died on 6 January 1972 in St Monica's Nursing Home in Belvedere Place, Dublin. She was in her late seventies. She is buried in Glasnevin cemetery in the same grave as Elizabeth O'Farrell who died before her. Their grave is near the republican plot but not in it, because to them, a republican plot meant one reserved exclusively for those, who, like themselves, would admit of no compromise with the republican ideal. It is beside the grave of Brian O'Higgins, who served with them in the GPO. It faces that of O'Donovan Rossa, a position chosen specially by Julia because of the association of Pádraig Pearse with Rossa.

Nora Connolly-O'Brien

Robert Lynd, in his introduction to *Portrait of a Rebel Father* by Nora Connolly-O'Brien, wrote that she had 'repaid love with love and pride with pride in a book that has been written from the depths of her remembering heart.' So it was, too, in her long chat with me. Her love for her father and her steadfast belief in the cause of freedom shone out even in these, her later years. She was, perhaps, the most willing talker among the women of the Revolution. Her voice was rich, with, here and there, strong echoes of Belfast. Her story as it unfolded was told quietly, but with passion. Her utter simplicity and candour were, quite unconsciously, full of artistry and skill. One was always aware that her words and her memories had been cherished and cultivated over the years. 'What we want here,' she said 'is truth; that only is important.'

I was conscious of the fact that here was a woman who was not only vividly aware of her own role in the Easter Rising, but also glowed with pride as she looked back to the days of her father, James Connolly. As she drew to the end of her story and brought me to that terrible night when she and 'Mama' visited her father for the last time I was unable to speak. The gigantic hero-figure of James Connolly lived and spoke through the eyes and voice of the woman who had, long ago, shared with him a unique moment of courage and sacrifice.

Nora Connolly-O'Brien

DONNCHA: What is your most vivid memory of your father at the time of the Easter Rising?

NORA: The only time I ever saw my father in uniform was on Easter Sunday morning and it was after I had given breakfast to all the signatories of the Proclamation. There he stood in the dark green uniform – I'd never seen him in uniform before – and I said to him, 'That's new', and he said, 'Yes, it's first-time on!' It fitted him beautifully and he looked grand in it. Then he put his sword-belt on and took the sword and I said, 'I must buckle that on for you!' I did so and he put his hands on my shoulders and said, 'Nora, you should be doing this for a young man and not an oldster like me,' and he smiled. He was so pleased that things were going right, that they all had come. He walked away from me, humming a song and then he burst out into the words: 'We've got another saviour now, that saviour is the sword.'

DONNCHA: I wonder is it possible to define the role of women in the Revolution. I get an impression of greater equality in 1916 than in later years. Was this the Citizen Army influence?

NORA: Well, yes. And even before 1916 when we were working up towards it, we were not compartmented. Women and men worked together as equals. We were accepted without any raising of eyebrows. It was everyone doing his or her best in any and every job that had to be done.

DONNCHA: Do you think that the women of 1916 were in any way special?

NORA: I think they were special in the way they responded to attitudes. Just as in the case of Margaret Skinnider. When they were going out to attack a nest of snipers she was in charge of the squad. William Partridge, a very famous man in the working-class movement, was there and he and other members of the squad accepted that she was in charge. This was more definite in the Citizen Army because the women in the army drilled with the men, listened to the same lectures and paraded together. The Volunteers were more inclined to be secretive and not to let the women of Cumann na mBan in on it. In the

Citizen Army the women knew everything that the men knew. That situation didn't develop after Easter Week. Women seemed to go back to their housewifely jobs, like looking after food and things like that and carrying messages - so-called non-dangerous jobs!

DONNCHA: Where were you, Nora, let us say in the middle of Easter Week?

NORA: I was outside Dublin at that time. I was sent to the North with various messages, hoping to get them out [to get sympathisers to rise out]. I spent most of the week frustrated. But I have some very pleasant memories as well. I remember being in Coalisland, in a hotel, and a man rushing in saying, 'Where are the first-aiders?' I stood up and he said, 'A man shot himself.' So I went over. The man had shot himself in the thumb and he was sitting there looking in amazement at his thumb! It wasn't serious, so I bandaged him up as all the men looked on in some awe. A man clapped me on the shoulder and said, 'You're the one for us!' I said, 'Fine, but how do you know but that I want to make holes, not plug them.' He smiled, 'Come with us and we'll let you do both!'

While we were waiting for the word [to rise out], the local organiser in Coalisland had gathered all his group in a big barn - and I stood still as it reminded me of all the things I'd read in books of the rendezvous of rebels. There they were, all around the walls, men sitting and waiting with their rifles and their bandoliers. It was extraordinary to see them there in the faint glimmer of a small oil lamp waiting for the word. They were all so quiet and serious. I'll remember the picture for ever! And the word, of course, never came.

DONNCHA: How did you get back to Dublin?

NORA: Well, we got as far as Dundalk and then we had to walk. My sister was with me. Ina and I started walking - there were only military on the trains. We spent the night in a field, shaking with the cold. We got near Balbriggan, exhausted and footsore. We went into a ploughed field, took off our shoes and stockings and plunged our poor feet into the rich, cool, brown earth and I think we dozed off because we were awakened by the thunder of gunfire. Off we went.

In Swords we were met by a platoon of British soldiers coming towards us. They had gun carriages and their rifles slung on their shoulders and they were marching in order. I said: 'Ina, Ina, they are marching away. Our men must be winning in Dublin!' And that is another picture that I carry in my mind. A success that seemed so possible, so real.

DONNCHA: But waiting for you in Dublin was a sad and brutal reality. When did you finally reach Dublin?

NORA: It must have been Saturday. We limped and walked in by Drumcondra and we decided we'd go to the home of the Ryans who lived on Clonliffe Road. We went along there and we were surprised to see many people standing at the doors and looking towards the city and there was a horrible smell of burning. The Ryans took us in and when they saw us unwashed and exhausted they were most kind.

DONNCHA: How did you get news of the Rising?

NORA: Of course the Ryans, when we asked them, one of them looked at us quietly and said in a rush, 'They're all surrendering!' 'My father?' I asked. 'Oh, he's wounded,' they said. 'He's dying,' they said. It took all the life out of us. We just sat there and couldn't talk. There was so much to think about — surrender, the fighting over and our father dying. I wondered if we would ever see him again, but of course Mama who had come down to Dublin from Belfast on Good Friday was now staying at Madame's [the Countess Markievicz] cottage at the Three Rock. She had the younger people with her there. Roddy went into the Post Office with my father, so he stayed with him.

DONNCHA: How was your mother reacting?

NORA: Well, I was thinking to myself - what will Mama do if she hears it like this. She'd be terribly worried. So, I said to Ina, 'We'll just have to make our way out to the Three Rock and get to Mama.' We walked across Dublin and there we saw what had happened. The soldiers let us through. We told them that we were looking for our mother and they waved us on without the necessary permit. O'Connell Street! Oh, it was

Destruction in O'Connell Street after the Rising.

terrible! All the buildings in ruins. We passed Cathedral Lane. There were dead horses lying there and that horrible smell of burning everywhere. The GPO was in absolute ruins but the flag was still flying. It lifted my heart and I said to Ina: 'Look, look, a complete ruin, yet the flag is still flying. That's a good omen.' We passed on.

In Rathmines we saw a poster for *The Daily Sketch* with a photograph of my father on it. 'The Dead Rebel Leader,' it said. I was hoping that Mama wouldn't have seen that.

DONNCHA: Arriving at Madame's cottage and meeting your mother must have been an emotional experience.

NORA: Indeed, it was. Even from outside we could hear weeping, deep sobs and frightened children crying. I went in and they were sitting there. Someone had brought her in a copy of the *Sketch* and the young ones were frightened when they saw Mama crying. I said: 'Mama, that's wrong. They have confused Daddy with Seán Connolly. Daddy is wounded, in hospital. We must find out where he is and go to see him.'

'Oh, I thought I'd lost everyone!' she said. 'You and Ina away. Daddy - I didn't know what happened to him and I haven't seen Roddy since he went off.'

Anyway, I got her to pack up a few things and come into Dublin and she was amazed. The extraordinary thing was, you know, that though we - that is Mama and I - accepted the fact that my father might be killed, we never expected defeat. So, we came into Dublin and went to stay with William O'Brien's family.

DONNCHA: How did you find out where your father was?

NORA: Well, we found out that he was being held in the Castle [Dublin Castle] and we asked to see him. I was to accompany Mama the first day and somebody told her she shouldn't bring me because the British were looking for me. Well, this was not so because I was not known at all in Dublin. Mama was frightened, so as she was so frightened I let her go and she took the youngest, Fiona, who was only about seven at the time, with her and they saw Daddy. Mama came back very despondent but still happy that he was alive and that she had seen him. They were very close, my father and mother.

DONNCHA: You visited him too?

NORA: I saw him twice before he was executed. As I said before, Mama and I thought that he might be killed in the fight but we never thought of defeat. So, we never thought of execution. It never entered our heads! And then came that awful, awful week in May when every morning the newsboys would come around with the 'stop press - two more executions', 'another execution', every day. Day after awful day, from May 3rd to May 12th. Any day that there were no executions those whose men were alive thanked God for it. We thought it was over then.

DONNCHA: But of course it had not ended.

NORA: Indeed no. For then it began again. It was an awful time. Dublin was very strange, being under martial law. Every street was paraded. You weren't supposed to have a light showing anywhere. You weren't allowed to have a window facing into the street open. If by chance you forgot and put a light in the room, you'd hear the English voices: 'Put out that light, put out that light.'

DONNCHA: There must have been an all-pervasive feeling of defeat too.

NORA: You were never free of it. You were never free of the power of the enemy that had defeated you. It was really terrible, people going around the streets trying to find this and do that. You helped where you could, listening to people's troubles.

DONNCHA: And now, Nora, what was it like when the sad moment of parting came?

NORA: I paid two visits to him. It is the last visit that I remember most. We were wakened at about half-past one in the morning by soldiers rattling on the door, and when we went down we were told that the prisoner, James Connolly, wanted to see his wife and his elder daughter. They had a car and offered to take us there. Mama was terrified. I said, 'We'll go and see anyway.' So we were driven through Dublin right up to the Castle. It was eerie going through the

James Connolly.

city. Nobody on the streets and still that horrible smell of burning. It was like the smell of water dropped on ashes. There were only soldiers to be seen.

We went into the Castle and were handed over to some other officer and he brought us into the room where there was a nurse. She called us away from the view of the keyhole. She said, 'I'm supposed to search you, but I'm not going to do it.'

'What has happened?' said Mama. 'I don't know anything,' said the nurse, but I could see that she was dreadfully upset. After a moment, by which time the search should have been over, there was a knock on the door and the soldier came in. He led us out and brought us up the central staircase which was lined on both sides by soldiers with fixed bayonets. Outside my father's door there were two soldiers.

When Daddy saw us, he smiled. 'Well Lily,' he said, 'you know what this means?' And she said, 'Not your beautiful life, James, not your beautiful life!' And she broke down. He patted her on the shoulder and he said: 'Haven't I had a great life, Lilian? Isn't this a good end?' But she broke down very much. He tried to pat her and he said, 'Don't cry, Lily, you'll unman me!' He said, 'I slept for the first time tonight and they wakened me to tell me I was to be executed at dawn. So then, I asked for you and Nora.' He was very calm.

Mama was really broken-hearted. I had a lump in my throat. He looked at me and he said, 'Well Nora, don't cry!' I said, 'No, no, I won't cry.' He tried talking to me, advising me about various things that we should do when he was gone, tried to keep it a businesslike kind of talk and then they knocked at the door and they said: 'It's time to come. Time's up!'

We couldn't move Mama away. She was rooted to the floor. My father said to me, 'Go help your mother, Nora.' And though he couldn't lift himself up in the bed, he couldn't lift his shoulders from the bed, he put his two arms around me and he said: 'Nora, girl, I'm very proud of you. Take your mother away, get your mother away.' I think he felt that he might lose control too.

So, the nurse came in and she and I, we both got Mama out and Mama seemed to get much calmer when she was away from Dada and we went down to the room again where the nurse had refused to search us and Mama asked her would she get a lock of his hair.

I never saw him again.

Biography

Nora Connolly shared the vicissitudes of her father's life to the full. When she was a small child he took her with him to political meetings in Dublin. Later, the family emigrated to America and Nora worked as a milliner in New Jersey. Then they moved to New York where Connolly founded the Irish Socialist Federation. He started a monthly journal *The Harp* and Nora became business manager, looking after the affairs of the paper while her father was away on his frequent lecture tours.

The Connolly's returned to Dublin in 1910. While canvassing during elections, Nora saw for herself the poverty and misery of the working classes living in the tenements. When she told her father how horrified she was by the conditions she had seen, he said to her: 'It is because of these things that we are working. We have to change all that.'

Later, the family moved to Belfast, where Nora worked in a warehouse. She organised the Belfast branch of Cumann na mBan and joined the girls' branch of the Fianna. With some friends she founded the Young Republican Party and designed and made their banner, a rising sun on a green background with the name of the party in white letters.

After the Howth gun-running in July, 1914, Nora was sent to America with a message to the heads of the movement there. 'Five people', her father told her, 'are in danger of being hanged if the message is discovered - one of them will be yourself.' Nora accomplished her mission successfully.

Another time she was sent to England to find Liam Mellows and bring him back to take part in the Rising. He had been deported from Ireland after a term of imprisonment. She found him near Stoke-on-Trent and arranged his return to Ireland disguised as a priest.

After Easter Week, 1916, Nora went to America and told the story of the Rising to huge, enthusiastic meetings. When she landed in England on her way home, she was served with an order forbidding her to go to Ireland. She records that the Lord Lieutenant wrote, 'It is utterly impossible and extremely inadvisable to allow you to return to Ireland.' She evaded the prohibition by disguising herself as a boy and hiding in the dark stuffy forecastle of a cargo steamer during its thirty-five hour passage across the Irish Sea.

She was active in the General Election of 1918 when Sinn Féin swept the country. Then came marriage not long before the Treaty of 1921 and imprisonment in Mountjoy and Kilmainham jails during the troubled times that followed.

The family of James Connolly knew poverty, hardship and tragedy at first hand. Nora Connolly-O'Brien looks back with pride at her father's accomplishments and at his sacrifice.

Leslie Bean de Barra

Leslie Bean de Barra was anxious to talk. Of all the people in this book she was the most conscious of history, of the need to keep and to document the important details.

When I first met her, she was a neat white-haired woman who looked you straight in the eye and answered your questions without prevarication or deviation. Her eyes would light up when conversation brought her over the history of her beloved Cumann na mBan or when the name of her husband, General Tom Barry, was mentioned.

Leslie wrote me a long letter before our interview and this brings a certain formality to what follows. She explained very clearly that her interest in being interviewed had nothing whatsoever to do with personal achievement. Instead, she saw it as a small contribution to recording the great role of women in the Easter Rising and in the War of Independence which followed.

She had a great desire to have a book written, a book which would deal accurately, though not necessarily sympathetically, with the role of Cumann na mBan. She was not tardy in pointing out that there were many other women who ought to be talked to and urged me to seek out Máire Comerford, Síghle Bean Uí Dhonnchadha, Julia Grenan, Nora Connolly-O'Brien and several others.

Members of Cumann na mBan who were active in 1916.

DONNCHA: Mrs Barry, you joined the national movement in 1915. Why?

LESLIE: My father and mother were strong Parnellites and when Parnell died their attention went to Sinn Féin around 1904. Then, in 1913, the Irish Volunteers started and two of my brothers joined the night it started at the meeting in the Rotunda. I was at the Dominican Training College in Belfast. Then I came to Dublin in 1915 and I joined Cumann na mBan.

DONNCHA: So your love of Ireland and your desire to serve began at home?

LESLIE: I was reared in a home where nationality was considered very highly, and my mother was a very keen nationalist. I remember when I came to Dublin - I had been in Belfast and John Redmond was considered to be the cat's whiskers up there - I got a picture of John Redmond from someone and one evening at home my mother took it, folded it and put it in the dustbin and then I realised that I had made a very severe faux pas.

We were not a very communicative family. My brothers didn't say anything to me about the Volunteers or Cumann na mBan or anything. But then, of course, we read everything, a great family of readers. It seems shockingly bad manners I suppose but every one of us sat down to our meals with a book in front of us, my mother included. We read an enormous amount and I suppose that was what helped us to understand. We didn't have to talk to each other about it.

But I remember well what made me join the Movement. It was on a Sunday in 1915 at the O'Donovan Rossa funeral. I was standing at the corner of the Mater Hospital on Berkeley Road and I saw the funeral coming by. I saw Tom Clarke, Pearse and all the Volunteers carrying rifles and I said to myself, this looks serious. It was the serious look of the men, and of course Pearse's oration at the graveside that did it. On the following Tuesday night I joined the Ard-Chroabh of Cumann na mBan in Parnell Square.

DONNCHA: Who received you into Cumann na mBan?

LESLIE: Mrs Tom Clarke. I had been a member of the Ard-Chraobh of the Gaelic League beforehand and it was in the same house. Mrs Tom Clarke was the President of the Ard-Chraobh of Cumann na mBan and Sorcha Mac Mahon was the Honorary Secretary.

DONNCHA: What were the first things you did in the Cumann?

LESLIE: In Cumann na mBan the first things we were taught were first aid and home nursing, and, of course, we were lectured and told all about the organisation. It was founded in November 1913 and was an independent organisation of women but closely associated with the Irish Volunteer movement. It has its headquarters in Harcourt Street; that was later to be the HQ of Sinn Féin. Then, in November 1914, the executive of Cumann na mBan declared its support for the Irish Volunteer Manifesto and as a result they lost some of the branches throughout the country. The loss was only temporary, for the organisation grew from strength to strength.

The Ard-Chraobh was the first branch in Dublin. It was thought that it would be better to divide Dublin into branches and to have a branch of Cumann na mBan immediately associated with a branch of the Irish Volunteers. There were four battalions of the Irish Volunteers in Dublin. Number 1 with its HQ in Blackhall Place. The Number 2 Battalion had its HQ in Fairview; Number 3 and 4 were south of the Liffey, around Donnybrook - the fourth was around Dev's area and the third was Eamon Ceannt's area, around by the docks.

*   *   *

DONNCHA: What were you doing prior to the Easter Rising?

LESLIE: We were very busy making field dressings and had extra classes in first aid and we also initiated the Defence of Ireland Fund - that was a collection for the army and the equipping of the Volunteers. That year we used to have concerts every other Sunday night and we organised a series of lectures also to procure funds. So, we were very busy.

We had no knowledge of the imminence of the situation.

Well, I suppose Mrs Clarke and those senior officers would have had, but the ordinary rank and file didn't. There was one thing, however, that struck me and gave me the idea that there was something serious coming off. On the eve of Palm Sunday there was a very large céilí organised in what's now called the Banba Hall and I remember quite well seeing Seán MacDiarmada and all those there, and I said to myself, 'tis extraordinary to see the whole lot together, and of course it was like a final reunion they were having.

The Thursday night previous to that Saturday I remember I left the Ard Chomhairle meeting and I was walking home. We lived on the North Circular Road and a lady, she's dead since, who was prominent in the Organisation said to me when we got to the Mater Hospital corner, 'You know, Leslie, the Rising is to take place on Sunday!' Well, of course, this nearly knocked me off my feet altogether. I realised that it was a frightful error on her part, to tell me, a very junior member of Cumann na mBan, and I didn't say a word to my two brothers. I didn't say anything at home. As I say, we weren't a family that communicated much with one another.

Then I remember on the Good Friday that there was great coming and going and on Easter Saturday my two brothers were out and around county Dublin gathering in arms and so on for their own men. Then it came to Easter Sunday morning and everyone was aghast at the countermanding order of Eoin MacNeill which was printed in the only Dublin paper of the time, the *Independent*. I think the men were taken aback more than anyone. But there was no discussion on it in my home. My eldest brother was captain of the Volunteers under Thomas MacDonagh and my other brother was in the First Battalion. I suppose they had discussions between themselves. I don't know. They didn't say anything!

About twelve o'clock on Easter Sunday I got a note from the Secretary of Cumann na mBan saying you weren't to leave home, you were to stand by for that day and the next day. I remember a cyclist, a courier, coming for my brothers probably with the same kind of note. I stayed at home. I didn't say anything and on Monday morning at about eight o'clock I saw the cyclist coming for my two brothers. At about ten o'clock I got a note to say that I was to report to the corner of Blessington Street leading towards the Black Church. I was mobilised for there. I put on my haversack and went up and a great number of our branch of Cumann na mBan were there. We were to report around eleven o'clock. We were to be attached to Ned Daly's Battalion which was occupying Church Street and the Four Courts. We were told to wait for instructions. We waited until nearly one o'clock.

I had a great friend, her name was Brid Dixon, the daughter of Henry Dixon who was one of the founders of Sinn Féin, and we stood talking for a bit and I said, 'I'm not going home today!' She said, 'Where are you going?' We had seen the lancers going down from the Phoenix Park, down Blessington Street, and they were all beautifully plumed. You never saw anything like them, you'd think they were going down to receive some royalty. Then we heard some firing. It was that really that made me say, 'I'm not going home today!' 'So,' Brid said. 'We'll go down to the GPO.' You see, we had heard it was occupied, so we went down and we went in and the first people we met were Tom Clarke and Seán MacDiarmada. We knew these very well. We saw other men that we knew and girls. Tom Clarke then said to the two of us, 'Stand by, because we're going to use the two of you as couriers.' He and Seán MacDiarmada were in a small office. I'd say that it would have been about four o'clock.

Tom Clarke came to me and said that there were men over in the Hibernian Bank at the corner of Abbey Street and they occupied that whole block and would I go over and take charge of Cumann na mBan in that building. I went across. That was Monday afternoon. We made tea for the Volunteers. They were from the Second Battalion and that night was kind of quiet.

By Tuesday, then, the British had occupied the roof of the Ballast Office and you see the corner of Abbey Street was a perfect target for them. And I think it was on Wednesday I was standing in one of the rooms at the corner. At the time I didn't understand anything of the nature of a military operation and Tom Weafer, God be good to him, he was from Wexford, he was in charge of the unit occupying the building. Just as I was standing alongside him at the window a bullet came in and caught him in the stomach. He fell down. I knelt down beside him. I knew of course that 'twas such a severe place that he was gone, that he was hardly going to live. So I did what I could for him and I realised that he was going to pass out and we knelt round him and said some of the Rosary, whispered an Act of Contrition into his ear, and he died within half an hour. On the Wednesday we got an instruction from the GPO and the instruction was to evacuate the building.

* * *

When it got dark Brid Dixon and I used to be sent with ammunition and with dispatches to Ned Daly in the Capuchin Hall in Church Street and we used to take messages back from him to Tom Clarke. We did that every night when it got dark. They broke cavities in the walls from the GPO to where Arnott's is now. We used to climb through those, come out at Arnott's and go down the street and up Mary Street and Mary's Lane into Church Street. We used to have great gabbing and talking I needn't tell you with Ned Daly and with any of the men or Cumann na mBan who might be there and we would bring back the messages. I remember the second night we were going out Seán MacDermott gave us two officer's canes - they have steel tops to them. He said, 'If anyone touches you, use that on them.'

Then we came back one night, I remember, and the commissariat was closed and we got nothing to eat and I said to Brid, 'I'm starving!' That was the beauty of the men at that time, you could say anything to them; you could say anything to Tom Clarke or Seán MacDiarmada. I saw Mick Collins there, God be merciful to him, and Gearóid O'Sullivan. So, I said: 'I'm starving with the hunger. I didn't get a cup of tea, the commissariat was closed except for officers.' 'We'll make them officers tonight now,' Seán MacDiarmada said to Tom Clarke, 'so they'll get their suppers!' We were made officers on the battlefield I always said afterwards.

The person who was in charge of the commissariat, the woman who was magnificent in Easter Week in the kitchens and the commissariat, was Louise Gavan Duffy. I'll never forget her. She was the greatest inspiration any woman or girl could have. She never got off her feet. I'd say she hardly got one hour's sleep during the whole week and the last that I saw of her, her feet were very swollen. So, she gave us our supper.

*   *   *

The next thing I remember now was Thursday in the middle of the afternoon and Tom Clarke called me and he said, 'You have to go over to Marlborough Street Church and bring back a priest.'

The tears were coming into my eyes with fear but I was ashamed to let them come down my cheeks before Tom Clarke. So I said, 'Very well.' I went out the side of the Post Office and got up Moore Street and across by the Rotunda, keeping in by the wall. Now at that time I knew that there was a barricade of British soldiers up at Findlater's Church and I said to myself, If I run now I'll be nipped off. So what I did was I walked very slowly to the foot of Parnell, looked up at him and I crossed to the other side of what was Britain Street and I came to the corner of Marlborough Street and I crept in by the railings of houses and all the women standing in the hallways were screaming, 'Go home girl, you'll be killed, because the British are in the Education Office!' But I knew I had to go on.

I went on and I got to the steps of the presbytery. With the heel of my shoe I battered on the door. I was shivering there and after a while a priest came out to me and said, 'Come down, we're down in the cellars.' I went down. He said, 'What do you want?' I said, 'I've been sent over from the General Post Office for a priest.' He looked at me and he said, 'Do you realise that you're working in there with a group of communists, that you have James Connolly and all the socialists in there?' So I said, 'I have been sent for a priest.' 'I'm certain no man or woman in the General Post Office wants a priest,' he said. I knew that every one of us had gone to confession on Easter Saturday, but I thought, if a man is dying, it is a consolation to have a priest. So I said, 'If you don't want to come, I'm going back and I'm going back alone.'

He considered for a bit and he talked still about the socialists and the communists and what not and he said: 'You're a very foolish child. You should be at home with your parents!' However I said, 'Well now I'm going.' So he said, 'We won't go out the front door, we'll go out the back.'

That was the street where Cathal Brugha was killed later, the Lord be merciful to him. We went up that and came to what is now Seán MacDermott Street. He said, 'We'll run across the street here.' We ran across to where Cranes, the piano makers, used to be and we crept along the sides of the houses and down Moore Street again. We got to the GPO and went in by the side door. I said, 'Goodbye, I'm handing you over now to Tom Clarke and Seán MacDiarmada.' I was delighted to be rid of him. I got him in at any rate.

However, I think he stayed for a time. I didn't see him afterwards, except that after I came home and when we were giving in our reports to our committee of Cumann na mBan I didn't mention anything about him. I thought, the man is alive now and I don't want the finger to be pointed at him. Let the Lord deal with him. But he had done what he was asked to do.

DONNCHA: How did you combat fear?

LESLIE: I don't think I ever realised that the situation was fearful and I don't even today. It's extraordinary. I don't think that I ever realised what fear was when I was in the thing. If I were outside, I probably would have been very dithery,

Leslie Bean de Barra with her husband Tom Barry.

imagining that everyone belonging to me and everyone I knew was killed.

* * *

In the Post Office there was great concern about the top floor. It had to be flooded with water - if an incendiary fell on the place this would help to stem its activity. Someone came to me and said, 'Your brother Seán is up there on the top floor since Tuesday.' I went up and I saw him. There were some of his own company - Dick Gogan, he's a Fianna Fáil TD now, and other men that I knew, and I was talking with them and then I said, 'I can't stay up here with ye.' They were sitting in pools of water.

* * *

On Friday, I suppose it would have been about twelve o'clock, we were called before Pearse and every one of us was told to line up. Pearse told us - he didn't say that it was the end or anything, but he said, 'We have to evacuate all of you and the best thing you can do is take our wounded to Jervis Street Hospital.' Some of us said that we wouldn't go, that we'd stay behind. Then we had a little huddle and a talk among ourselves. We decided we'd only be an encumbrance on the men - that if they had to evacuate that they'd be, kind of, staying back to protect us.

DONNCHA: It all seems very democratic.

LESLIE: It was absolutely democratic. We had such common feeling with them. We knew we would only be a burden to them if they were trying to escape out of that small door in Henry Street.

Miss Gavan Duffy was put in charge of us. We were let out by the side door of the Post Office and we took the wounded up to Jervis Street hospital and then we realised we'd only be in the way there. So, at the corner of Capel Street looking down Mary Street there was a barricade of British soldiers and we were called up there by the officer. The officer-in-charge, I suppose 'twas an NCO, said to take us up to Broadstone, that we were prisoners. So we were marched off up there and on the way, you see, Louise Gavan Duffy had whispered to some of the others and 'twas passed down to some of us who knew the nuns in Eccles Street, that when we'd be brought before the military for questioning at Broadstone that we would say we were students from the school, that we had been out for a walk down O'Connell Street and we were ordered to go into the General Post Office. So we were brought in one by one and some of us spun this story, and it was taken, accepted, and then we were told, 'Well, you can go back to the school.' So I needn't tell you we did march back to Eccles Street in case anyone was behind us. When we got in there the nuns gave us tea and we were able to go home.

DONNCHA: Was Pearse sad when he told you to leave the GPO?

LESLIE: He was. He was the type of man now that you hardly ever saw him smile. His eyes would light up when he was pleased, and of course I attended lots of lectures given by him in what was called the Ancient Concert Rooms in Brunswick Street. He would throw back his head and close his eyes and the words would flow from him. It was beautiful to listen to his voice, his ideas. He was very, very quiet.

*   *   *

DONNCHA: You talked a good deal about Tom Clarke. Did you like him?

LESLIE: I really think that Tom Clarke was the best man that Ireland ever produced. Now I'm saying in the past - we must remember that I have a husband, but he, like myself, thinks that Clarke was wonderful. For a man to have spent fifteen years - a shocking situation - in an English jail and then to have come back and heartened everyone! The great thing about Tom Clarke, and it's the great thing that people of the age-group of forty to sixty should remember now, was that we would never have been so faithful except for the effect Tom Clarke had on us. I remember before the Rising, you know, I would be sent to his shop in Parnell Street with messages or dispatches and he'd always bring you in and talk to you as if you were an adult and he trusted us so much that we couldn't but react to that trust by giving him trust and faithfulness afterwards.

The last person I saw coming out of the Post Office was Tom Clarke and he shook me by the hand and he said, 'If you see my wife —' and he stopped for a minute and he continued, 'Tell her the men were wonderful to the . . .;' and then he stopped and said goodbye, and I knew he meant 'end'. I could see that he was very pent up, but I was very, very proud of the fact that they had held out for the week.

* * *

DONNCHA: What an extraordinary time it was to be young.
LESLIE: It was wonderful in this way - and I always thank God for letting me live in that generation - wonderful, the equality of men and women. We didn't have to have any 'women's lib.' at all at that time. Men accepted us for what we were worth and all through the 'Tan' time women had never to say, 'I'm a woman.' We knew they'd protect us in any way. They let us talk out our views, quite easily, and we were absolutely equal, except, of course, that we didn't fight as they did but we never had to feel that we wanted any rights because we had the rights through our own good will and through our willing help for them.
DONNCHA: Following 1916, after the executions, the imprisonments and the general re-awakening, Cumann na mBan were really carrying on the Revolution on their own, weren't they?
LESLIE: Yes, they were. They were wonderful. They all came together. The first few weeks afterwards it was a case of going up to Richmond Barracks with parcels and food and clothing for the men because we knew that they'd be deported and imprisoned. We did what we could for them.

Every day the paper carried an announcement of another shooting, another execution and, of course, that was very depressing. But the leaders of Cumann na mBan, I must say, were wonderful women. The widows of all the executed men were splendid. They rallied us all together and they started a Prisoners' Dependants Fund. Tom Clarke had left some small amount of money with Mrs Clarke for her and then we organised collections and we re-vitalised Cumann na mBan and it grew from strength to strength.

DONNCHA: One gets an impression of serious dedicated young women but there must have been, now and again, a lighter side to things.

LESLIE: We never missed a céilí and we had outings to the mountains. Of course the bicycle was the real thing at that time. We re-organised Cumann na mBan in the city and we developed a council of representatives from all the branches. We worked through the country too.

After 1917 the work in the country was intensified and I became the Director of Organisation and I went through the country organising Cumann na mBan branches. I had the time of my life I can tell you.

DONNCHA: Is it possible to say how the country and the country women reacted to you?

LESLIE: Well, the reaction at first of course - well you must remember that quite a number of boys and men had joined the British Army and their relatives were dependent on allowances from the British Government and they were very, very hostile at the beginning. But I'd say the executions, really, made them realise the situation. Then there was a very great swing to Sinn Féin and the Volunteers. Then, of course, the majority of the Volunteers were released from Frongoch and they came home at Christmas 1916 and January 1917 and they started their re-organisation right through the country too.

* * *

DONNCHA: Inevitably, one hears a good deal of the Countess

Markievicz and Maude Gonne. Did you meet either?
LESLIE: She [the Countess] was the President of Cumann na mBan. I'd met her once or twice before 1916 itself but then immediately after 1916 there was the Convention of Cumann na mBan held in the autumn and I was elected on to the executive and then I got to know her very well, because she presided at all our meetings. Mrs MacBride I didn't know; she was of course out of Ireland until after 1916. I had met her in 1903 or 1904, I'm not sure. A King or Queen, which was it?, came to visit Dublin and the Castle authorities decided they would have all the loyal children go to the Phoenix Park for a party and Seán MacDiarmada and Tom Clarke and all those – and I think Mrs MacBride was in on this also, and Madame [the Countess] – they decided that all the children of nationalist families would have a party in Clontarf Park. It was summertime and my mother took us all down there and we got all sorts of cakes and jam and lemonade. It was an anti-royalist party.

* * *

DONNCHA: Looking back now over all the years, how important was Cumann na mBan to the national movement?
LESLIE: I think it was absolutely essential in this way that it established that women are a part of the nation and that if a man is willing to defend his country, a woman should be ready to defend it, by any means in her power. Well the only power that we had was to be an auxiliary during a time of operations and that held right through the country during the 1916-21 period and up to 1923.

You see, Cumann na mBan were always there to have shirts and everything ready for the men going into action and, of course, you must remember that one woman showed what a woman's part can be and I'm glad to say 'twas a woman in Cork. She saved the name of Cork for all time – Mrs Kent from Bawnard near Fermoy. Her four sons were in the house. She lay on the floor beside them at the windows and she emptied their rifles and refilled them as they needed them. You see, there the woman was established as a defender, completely.

Biography

One of the striking features of the Rising of 1916 and the War of Independence that followed was the part played by the courageous women of Cumann na mBan. Some, like the Countess Markievicz and Margaret Skinnider, took an active part in the fighting in Easter Week. Dr Kathleen Lynn served as medical officer with the battalion in the College of Surgeons. Others, like Louise Gavan Duffy, stayed in the General Post Office all that week, helping the fighting men in every way they could. Most of them acted as auxiliaries, having been specially trained in nursing and first aid. A small number were given the dangerous duty of carrying dispatches from post to post. Among these was Leslie Price, later Bean de Barra.

After the Rising she became Director of Organisation for Cumann na mBan and travelled throughout the country, helping to organise the resistance movement. In this way she met General Tom Barry, leader of the West Cork Flying Column and a legendary hero of the war against the Black and Tans. They were married in 1921.

He took the republican side on the Civil War and was imprisoned in the Curragh for a while. Later, the Barrys settled in Cork, where he was appointed a general superintendent with the Cork Harbour Commissioners in 1927. From the thirties on, they seemed to hold themselves aloof from the political establishment, although the General never wavered in his republican beliefs and allegiance. After the turmoil of the revolutionary years, his wife devoted the rest of her long life to service in the relief of human suffering at home and around the world.

She was a member of the Irish Red Cross Society from its inception in 1939 and became chairwoman in 1950. She was decorated by the Irish, German, Italian and Netherlands governments for her outstanding service to the Society and in 1978 received the International Committee's highest award, the Henri Dunant Medal. She was also national president of Gorta until her resignation in 1968, an active worker in the Gaelic League and chairwoman of the Erinville Hospital for five years. The National University of Ireland conferred the honorary degree of LL.D. on her.

General Tom Barry died in July 1980 and his passing revived memories of his heroic early days, notably the famous ambush of Black and Tans at Kilmichael. His wife was then in her late eighties and in poor health. She died on 9 April 1984 aged ninety-one.

Father Patrick Peyton

I first met Fr Peyton, 'The Rosary Priest', in Ballycastle, Co. Mayo, during the making of a series of 'Donncha's Travelling Roadshow' for television. To say that I and the rest of the TV crew were impressed would be to understate. Startled, surprised, moved are other expressions that readily spring to mind.

Fr Peyton dominates. His arrival on the set unheralded soon had us on our knees - an unfamiliar position for many - as he calmly recited a decade of the Rosary. There was no gainsaying the man. His technique was simple and direct: 'Let us pray now to Mary, Our Holy Mother, for the guidance and blessing of her Divine Son in the work which we are about to undertake.' Unwilling knees were soon bent!

His belief in God, in the Son of God and in Our Lady, are striking and terrifying. He has, quite literally, moved and addressed millions all over the world. He has boundless confidence and a humble awareness of his own role. Unlike many other evangelists there is nothing of the spiritual superstar about Fr Patrick Peyton. His power, and power he has, is quietly mirrored in his unwavering gaze, in the strength of his handshake and in what seems to be an internal and constant colloquy with the Divine. He rarely finishes a sentence without some reference to God or the Blessed Virgin.

He draws a deep strength from the unbending faith of his Mayo ancestors. When you ask him to look back towards the older Patrick Peyton, his father, you are made startlingly

Fr Patrick Peyton.

aware of the undying continuity of a simple faith. Fr Peyton is both easy and difficult to talk to: easy in that he is willing to answer any and every question, but difficult in that he seems enmeshed in his own constant interior spirituality and will, if you are not careful, lose himself in it.

Fr Patrick Peyton is unique in our time. He stands erect in his twilight years, a giant and old-fashioned Leviathan of Irish spirituality. He is, as I've said, unique among our voices.

 FR PEYTON: I feel that I'm the King of the Tinkers -but for our Holy Mother's sake and service, always to serve her, to get consciences and minds aware of that precious woman that God chose to give to us our redeemer.

DONNCHA: Fr Peyton, let's take you back, many miles and many roads to childhood in Mayo. Where were you born?

FR PEYTON: In a little place called Carracastle near Ballina and near my mother's parish, Bunnyconnellan.

DONNCHA: What did your father do?

FR PEYTON: Well, my father, really, was a small farmer with about twelve acres of land. It wasn't enough to feed the nine children he had so he had to go to England and work. I think that he was a handyman - a bricklayer or a stonemason. I don't know if he went to the hay and the harvesting and the picking of potatoes in England as most of our neighbours did at that time when I was growing up. He scraped together enough money to keep us alive.

DONNCHA: What are your earliest memories of home?

FR PEYTON: My earliest memory of home is the one that I can never forget: the evenings when my mother and father knelt beside each other with the Rosary beads in their hands and my older brothers and sisters - I was the sixth - on their knees there. That is the beautiful thing that has so impressed itself on me. What it was then, what it did for us, what it is capable of doing for any family that would forget and turn out all their problems and be alone with God, and express to him their realisation of his very reality and ask the Blessed Virgin Mary to help them and to pool her beautiful spiritual influence with them as they asked her and asked her, 'Pray for us'.

That is, I feel, the real, real, important memory I have carried from county Mayo to any and every place, whether in universities, seminaries or wherever - that's the greatest thing that I can think of, remember or evaluate as the greatest gift that God gave me: to be born to that mother and father.

DONNCHA: During the family Rosary, did you take the decades in turn?

FR PEYTON: No. My father was the one who absolutely led it from beginning to end. That's what I loved, that it was he who led the family in the adoration and the praise of God. That was what the Rosary meant to me then and now.

DONNCHA: Were you aware as a young lad that times were hard?

FR PEYTON: Do you know, I wasn't! That's what is so beautiful. God is so wonderful that He fills the minds of those in trouble so that no matter how bad the trouble is it is supportable. You have no measure either of what would be easier to carry. So, I didn't realise that I was, maybe, living in poverty or destitution if we compare it with today. It was the best blessing I ever had, to be that way.

DONNCHA: Did you live far from school?

FR PEYTON: No, I walked to school. Beaufield school was the place and it was at the end of our fields almost. In five minutes we'd be at school.

DONNCHA: Do you remember your teachers? Were they important to you?

FR PEYTON: They were important. The first one was, maybe, the most important - the teacher for the infants' class - because, like a mother and father, her innocence and her spirituality left such an impression on the tiny little Pat Peyton that I worshipped her. She was a single woman, Miss

Maria Loftus. She, probably, supported my father and mother's responsibilities by impressing indelibly on me the one and only value worth keeping in mind: that God is real, that He is lovable and that He created us and died for us.

DONNCHA: How old were you when you left that school?

FR PEYTON: When I had left that school I had probably entered on the seventh class and then I transferred to a neighbouring school and after a few months there I finished. My father and mother had this beautiful wish that I wouldn't be destined to be a stone-breaker at the side of the road, or to plough the little fields, or dig the bog. They wanted me, they wanted all of the nine, to be something. But my father used to say, 'Pateen will never amount to anything.' And so, I wanted to be free from the school and the books and the learning. I finally got my way, because God is so nice that he gives you enough rope to hang yourself if you don't take the nice way. So, I got freedom.

I can never understand how my father allowed me, a kid of nineteen, to go to America and leave the controlling discipline and guidance that he exercised over me. He gave me freedom in one afternoon. I was weeding turnips with my brother in the little field. My father, in his sickness and illness, was sitting in the ditch watching his two sons. All of a sudden he consented and I can never understand it. We had thought to ask him to allow us go to England to work with the hay and the harvesting but he said, 'I'd rather let you go to America. Your three sisters are there to guard you.'

*   *   *

DONNCHA: Can you tell us about your last night in Ireland? What sort of farewell was it?

FR PEYTON: Well, it's a beautiful thing that is for me, also a lasting sureness of how Our Lady doesn't take her friends for granted, that she responds. It was that constant reciting over and over again of her Rosary that produced in my father that special response. Here he was to see his nineteen-year-old son off the next day. It was on a Sunday night when he gave me his last advice. There was only my mother, himself and me at the kitchen fire. Quietly, he said, 'Will you come with me to the room?'

Now, there was no electric light, there was no light at all in this room. He asked me to kneel down and on the wall was a picture of the Sacred Heart that was loved in our house. He looked at that picture and said, 'Watch over my son. Guard him. He's leaving me.' He said it - maybe not in those words - but he addressed Our Lord first. Then he addressed me. I was on my knees, with that tall man standing beside me in the dark, speaking with love and peace, telling me my responsibilities - that I was leaving home, that I would be on my own and then saying this beautiful line: 'Be faithful to Our Lord in America.'

That line was my father's farewell, a father who, through poverty, had to allow a nineteen-year-old son follow four others to leave him forever, never to see him again in this life. He wasn't worried about how I would make out financially in America, whether I might amass money or have a nice house and a business!

'Be faithful to our Lord in America' is an expression of love coming from a father, so loving God that he put God far and away ahead of me. All he was worried about was that I wouldn't hurt God, that I wouldn't be a traitor. My father branded me, he put a fiery thing into my mind with that line: 'Be faithful to Our Lord in America.'

*   *   *

DONNCHA: Now can we take you to America. How did you get there?

FR PEYTON: First we went in the train from Ballina Station. My brother and I went. The last sight I had of my father was when I was ready to turn that little part of the road where a hill would separate our house from the view. I looked back and who did I see looking over the half-door, looking towards that part of the road that would pull us forever from his sight as long as this earth lasted, but himself, looking with sadness and longing - his beautiful farewell that spoke more than a million words to me.

But now, at the station in Ballina was my mother. I got into the train with my brother and as the train pulled away she reached out to me with the love that she had for us and she raised a little handkerchief. The train pulled around a bend and I would never see her again. My heart almost broke that day, with sadness, with crying. The little white handkerchief was the signal that there was a woman holding it that I owed my life to.

DONNCHA: And that was the end of that period in your life?

FR PEYTON: That was the farewell to Mayo.

DONNCHA: How long did the journey to America take?

FR PEYTON: Well, we went down to Cobh and on the way we stopped at a thousand little stations to pick up more emigrants and more emigrants - the crying and the farewells made an impression on my mind. But we arrived finally at Cobh and got into a little hotel. Some miles earlier all the representatives of the hotels were pulling us by the coat tails when the train stopped saying come to us, others saying no, come to ours. So it was really like a cattle fair. I don't know what hotel we went to but the next morning we looked out and the last thing I saw was that beautiful spire of that church [Cobh Cathedral] as the tender brought us out to the big ship.

DONNCHA: A sad moment.

FR PEYTON: The last farewell was that beautiful house of God, a last farewell to a country that I love, that gave me my faith, that gave me my love for God and Mary. That is the memory I have of the last sight of Ireland.

DONNCHA: What was the ship like?

FR PEYTON: Well, the ship - the Lord bless us I cannot think of it except that I was bashful, I was shy, in fact I feel the poor little sailors who were sophisticated laughed at the poor little Peyton because my pants were shorter than they should be. The experience on the ship is blurred to me, except that it was foreign and it was strange.

DONNCHA: Did you have much money?

FR PEYTON: Oh Lord no. I don't know how much, but I entrusted it to a Molly Howley who was going to America with my brother - they meant to marry, I think. I entrusted the little money I had to her to guard for me in case it was stolen or lost, because we didn't have much money. My brother and Molly Howley didn't get married. He became a priest instead.

* * *

DONNCHA: How did the skyscrapers of New York compare with the little fields in Mayo?

FR PEYTON: Well, I thought that heaven couldn't compare with America. I saw, for the first time, electric lights in that little Scranton city where our neighbours from Mayo, a lot of them, were and where my three older sisters were. So, I arrived in Scranton, Pennsylvania. I saw electricity, I saw the whirling of signs and all the rest - the commercial signs -well I thought it was like fairyland. I thought heaven couldn't be anything like it.

The third oldest sister, Nellie was her name, knew so well, and so did the other two, that I was so longing to be a priest and a missionary as a young child serving Mass.

DONNCHA:When you were a young boy, you talked of this, I presume?

FR PEYTON: Oh yes. There was a lovely parish priest called Fr Roger O'Donnell who also wanted to help me reach my goal to be an African missionary. But when I grew to be a teenager and knew what it meant to be a priest - the price you'd pay to be a priest - I began to say, I'm not able to pay that price. It's not money, but the discipline, the prayerfulness, to be worthy to be another Christ for those whom you serve. I began to think I can not pay that price. So I began to shy away from the thought and try to get it out of my mind. I finally did, but with a great struggle.

But when I arrived in America what is the first thing that I'm told - because God doesn't give up either - my sister

Nellie said: 'Fr Kelly of the Cathedral of Scranton wishes to see you the first Sunday after you arrive. I've already made the appointment.' Well, that was the worst news I could get. That deflated my joy at seeing all the beautiful things in that city and I said to myself, the battle is going to start again; I'm not going to see him, it's the best way to avoid it. I refused to see Fr Kelly. Nellie expressed her disappointment, not in words but in a sadness that covered her face.

*   *   *

So, off I went looking for work. It is 1928. The Depression is coming to America. Nobody has a job for me. I travel for two weeks searching high up and low down for a job - any job, any place, and always: Sorry, sorry. In the meantime, Fr Kelly got in touch with my sister and said, 'Why did you not show up?' And she was so noble she didn't blame me. He said, 'Bring him down now.' So by that time I was glad to go down. Luckily, he didn't speak about the priesthood. He spoke instead about giving me a job. That pleased me, disposed me to continue listening. And what would the job be? To be the janitor of the Cathedral. They called it a nicer name: the sexton.

I would get the key, I would open that house of God in the dark of the winter mornings in 1928, clean up the furnaces, warm it up. Nobody is around, I'm alone with the Blessed Sacrament. At night I lock it. It's wintertime of '28, everybody is gone and I'm now alone with the Blessed Sacrament. And the longing began to take hold of me: Our Lord is alive, He's lovable, why don't you give yourself totally to His way?

That began to grow to such a degree that in a few months I dropped everything I was doing - I know well what I was doing: painting behind the main altar of the Cathedral. I left everything there and came around, genuflected, out the door and up to the priest's house, knocked at Fr Kelly's door and said I wanted to be a priest. And he said: 'What's a noun? What's a verb? What's an adjective?' I could answer fast. He

Fr Peyton talking to Donncha O Dúlaing.

said: 'Go over to the brothers across the street. Register for first year high school tomorrow. I'll pay your way. Tell your brother to leave the coal mines and sweep the church in your place. It will be safer. He may get killed in the mines.'

My brother left the coal mines and began to sweep the church and a month later joined me. Both of us kept on cleaning the church to pay our way and went to school at the same time. The Holy Cross priests, a great community of men, gave a mission in the Cathedral at the end of our first year high school. I was so impressed as I saw the Cathedral fill with the parishioners drinking in with their souls what those four missionaries were giving them about God and about being good, about what was ennobling and what was degrading, and I began to say, those are the men I want to be like. And my brother said the same. Fr Kelly was so noble as to say: 'I'll not stand in your way. Go out to Notre Dame, Indiana, the great place of the fighting Irish in the football teams.'

So that is where I was studying, that is where I prepared to become forever a priest and a religious, a man with vows. It meant thirteen years of training.

Eleven of the years went well. Then my health broke completely with TB [tuberculosis]. They got the doctor for me in the middle of the night because my lungs were bleeding so badly. The next morning an ambulance took me to the hospital. For three months I'm in that hospital without standing on my feet. Finally, I'm able to be moved back to Indiana where our mother house was. Now I'm placed in the infirmary with the old priests and the old brothers who have done their work and are waiting their turn to go home. I'm about thirty then and I see myself and all the dreams I had are down. The castles I had built are gone. I'm an invalid now and crippled. And I finally reach the stage when the doctors agree with me and say: Give up the treatment we are doing for you, it is useless, and trust in prayer.

So I had the option. I came back, closed the door of my little room, and really the tears fell down and I said I'm at Calvary at last. But Our Lord was at Calvary once and Easter was around the corner, and it was almost a parallel – my Easter was just around the corner. A knock came to the door. It was maybe the next night. When I say come in, there standing in that doorway is the one messenger from God that could do what that man did for me that night – one of the teachers I had at Notre Dame, Fr Cornelius Haggerty, whose ancestors came from Ireland. He stands beside my bed to beg me: 'Ask our Blessed Mother to cure you. She is alive. She is as real as your mother. She will be as good to you as you think she is. If you think she is a hundred-percenter, she will be. We limit her by our confidence. If we think she is a fifty-percenter, she will surely be that.'

He spoke like that with such depth and I was taking it all in as a child would, believing everything he said, knowing well Mary could not forget that since I could open my mouth in that little house in Mayo I united my voice with my sisters and brothers and my mother and father to say, Mary, your son is my God. I let the neighbours hear me say it as I said those Holy Marys in answer to my father saying it. And she couldn't forget it. So now I'm crying out to her: 'Mary, cure me. I believe you're alive. I believe your holy son could never say no to you if you ask him. Help this boy that is here, sick, and trusting in you.' She answered me, asked her son for me and my health began to come back.

First my depression went away. The darkness in my mind – the despair, the sorrow, the fears – all began to clear away, like the dawn begins to come and then the sun comes out and the day is here and the doctors say, pack your little suitcase and go back to your brother in the seminary. And I'm not describing a miracle. I shy from the word. They are not our criteria for believing – miracles – but the reality of Jesus and Mary of Nazareth. That was all I needed and the Rosary taught me that.

*   *   *

DONNCHA: Now we have come, obviously, to the Rosary campaign and the crusade. Let us strike one of the big chords first - you are as well known in Hollywood, I'm told, as you are in Mayo. How did you first come in contact with Hollywood?

FR PEYTON: Do you know, the real answer is nothing other than Our Lord's. When I wanted to say thanks I asked Him to show me how. And all of a sudden the thought came to me! Get every home doing what you lived in that little house in Mayo. You will find the answer to our family problems.

I knew immediately that that was how I would spend my life. Now I know what I have to do. But then I went to the Blessed Sacrament and said, I cannot do this, they will laugh me out of the pulpits, but you can and I'm asking you for ten million American families and every Catholic home in the world to be won over to this concept.

DONNCHA: This was your first target, ten million American families.

FR PEYTON: American families, that was my first target. But then to reach out to every Catholic home in the world. I placed that in the hands of the Blessed Sacrament. I could not do it. I couldn't even win one. I couldn't win a seven-year-old child, but dear Lord, I believe you are here. I'm asking you as a gift for your mother and mine.

He answered, because he gave me the Hollywood stars. It was as if the heavens had opened to give me the means to make the world aware - not just to make one little parish aware, but the world! To make it become a little village. He gave me the stars of Hollywood, every one of them - Jews, Protestants, Catholics - from the highest down.

DONNCHA: Who were they, Father? Can you recall the names?

FR PEYTON: Well, Bing Crosby was the number one. Loretta Young, Irene Dunne, Pat O'Brien, Gregory Peck, Ethel Barrymore, Joe E. Brown, Ann Blythe, Jeanie Craine.

DONNCHA: A good start! How did you use them? In what way were they essential to your work?

FR PEYTON: I first knocked at their doors. I said, I want to have you with me to such a degree that when I go back from

Hollywood to New York the networks will give me prime time.

DONNCHA: Coast-to-coast?

FR PEYTON: Coast-to-coast. If I have your names on a little piece of paper, I said, which says that you will appear whenever I will ask you, I am going to get the time.

I got thirty of them in the month of August. But that month of August was the month the atom bomb fell in Japan. So there is a connection between the disintegration of our civilisation and our world with this beautiful idea of a family that is the nucleus and strength of the world, or its weakness.

DONNCHA: What did you do on this programme?

FR PEYTON: I got about thirty of the biggest stars signing this little piece of paper for me. I went back to New York and met the president of the Mutual Broadcasting System, the biggest radio network that had about four hundred stations in its affiliate - television wasn't even thought of then - and we made a compromise. They said, we'll give you half-an-hour of prime time on this coast-to-coast Network and you will give us four things: a Hollywood star on that weekly half-hour programme, one at least; you will make it non-sectarian so that Protestants, Jews, anybody and everybody will benefit from it with the idea of family prayer instead of family Rosary; thirdly, you will pay the production costs; and fourthly you will make it a first-class programme.

These were the conditions and I went out to Hollywood with them. Loretta Young took me to her heart. She took her husband to task, saying: 'You are getting about fifty thousand dollars a year - and that was away back in '45 - to do what Fr Peyton wants. I want you to take him under your wing and fix this programme so that the stars will really be used to the utmost for the benefit of the homes of Americans and for the satisfaction of that Mutual Network that is trusting you so much as to give half-an-hour every week of prime time.' That is how the programme came into existence, the programme that glorified 'The family that prays together, stays together.'

DONNCHA: That was the great quote, wasn't it?

FR PEYTON: That was the quote. And there was another: 'A world at prayer is a world at peace.' But for me this is first: if you have a family praying you have a world at peace.

So, that is how we got started in Hollywood. After that the bishops took me in because I was glamourised then. I had a programme again, thanks to that dear God of whom I had once asked the question, Show me how? I had a plan for a bishop who would organise all his priests so that there would be only one voice for a period of three months from every pulpit; organise the teachers so that from every classroom, reaching to innocent little children would be the state of the family, the meaning of the family, the value of the family and the need of God's presence in the family if they hope to cope with today's world.

DONNCHA: What was the biggest crowd you ever addressed?

FR PEYTON: I'd say, according to the papers, São Paolo, Brazil. Two million, that's what they say. I'd say myself that it made no difference whether it was two million or two people. There was a multitude so great it was like a sea of people. Manila was the same. Madrid was the same. Rio de Janeiro was the same. Barcelona was the same. A million and a half were at some. Five hundred thousand attended others. At San Francisco there were five hundred thousand. There was no stadium. It was the Golden Gate Park, twelve miles of buses, back to back, policemen with helicopters organising the traffic.

DONNCHA: Your message has spread right around the world.

FR PEYTON: Yes. I'm on the road like a gipsy of Our Lady.

Biography

Father Patrick Peyton, the 'Rosary Priest', was born in Carracastle, near Ballina, Co. Mayo, in 1909. He tells Donncha O Dúlaing of his early life, his emigration to the United States, how be became a priest of the Holy Cross order and how he started his crusade to have the Rosary recited by families at home each night.

He persuaded Hollywood stars to participate in making family Rosary tapes and these became best sellers in America.

He has returned to Ireland many times and in 1954, the Marian Year, launched his Family Rosary crusade here. In 1977 at a press conference in Dublin, it was put to him that manufacturers of rosary beads had said that their sales had fallen since Vatican Council II, but Father Peyton refused to be daunted by this report.

In July 1978 it was reported that he was very seriously ill in the Good Samaritan hospital in Los Angeles, suffering from a massive heart blockage. He already had had four coronary bypasses inserted to correct a ninety per cent heart blockage and more surgery was now required. In February of the following year he visited Dublin and said that he had fully recovered from that illness, a recovery he attributed to the intercession of the Blessed Virgin Mary.

He told a press conference that he preached the message of prayer to the Blessed Virgin to thirty million people in five continents and that he had achieved his aim of having the Rosary recited nightly in ten million American homes. He had had an audience in Rome with the Pope, who had promised his full support to the Rosary crusade. Among his friends and helpers he had counted Bing Crosby and said that when Crosby died at the end of 1977 on a golf course at Madrid, he had in his pocket a rosary beads which had been given to him by Fr Peyton. Unlike the men and women who found religious orders, priests like Fr Peyton have no guarantee that their work will be continued after they are gone. It is peculiarly their own, inspired and directed by them personally. Their consolation must be the good they feel they have done in the society in which they lived and worked.

Siobhán McKenna

Siobhán McKenna is for many the authentic voice of theatrical Ireland. Like macLiammóir, McMaster or Cusack she stands apart, at the strange crossroads between being a legend in her own time and being still an active and creative practitioner in the theatre.

Paris, New York, Galway, Dublin and London have all played host to Siobhán McKenna. Yet she has in many ways eschewed the glamour and the wealth of an international career to remain at home with her own people, her own theatre, her own Ireland.

One tends, somehow, to hear her past through the soft cadences of Galway, whether in Irish or in English, but if one really listens with care one hears a slight, very slight, Northern flavour and this is not without good reason. It is there she has her roots.

 DONNCHA: Siobhán, what is your earliest memory?

SIOBHÁN: Well, my earliest memory of course would be of Belfast, which I remember very vividly although I left it when I was five years of age. I remember, now you have thrown that question at me,

Siobhán McKenna.

letting a pot of jam drop! I loved my mother and I used to help her go shopping - this was in Clonard Gardens, although I was born in St James's Park off the Falls Road. I think I remember the pot of jam because we were very poor. My father was a lecturer at Queens University and he also taught at the Tech. But the pot of jam sticks in my mind because that was a very special treat and I remember being aghast. I can still see the corner where it happened and I was carrying this pot of jam and my mother didn't give out to me.

DONNCHA: Was childhood a golden time for you?

SIOBHÁN: Golden. I have no unhappy memories except for my dogs dying, you know. They were my great griefs in childhood.

DONNCHA: Earliest memories of school, how do they strike you?

SIOBHÁN: Well, my earliest memories of school were at the Dominican Convent, Belfast. There I was in infants. I remember I did a lot of raffia work and embroidery work. And at the age of four I made an evening handbag for my mother which she used frequently when she went out. I have affectionate memories of Belfast and all my little friends.

DONNCHA: Your first impressions of Connacht?

SIOBHÁN: It was a miracle that we went to Connacht because it totally fired my imagination. I already spoke Irish in Belfast because my father brought a girl from Baile an Fheirtéirigh [Ballyferriter] so that we would have Irish.

There is a very funny story about that. The girl came up to help my mother and my father discovered that she had brains. So, my mother ended up cleaning her shoes while my father taught her Latin, French, mathematics. She had only been to national school but she won a scholarship to Galway University.

But when I arrived in Galway I remember in the Dominican Convent there new children had to get up and recite a poem. So, I recited a poem which I still remember,

> I met a little elfman once,
> Down where the lilies grow.
> I asked him why he was so small,
> And why he didn't grow.
> He smiled at me and with his eye,
> He looked me through and through,
> 'I'm quite as big for me,' said he,
> 'as you are big for you.'

Now the Galway children collapsed with laughter so I thought I was a huge success as a comedian, but of course they were laughing at my Belfast accent. It was the only accent I had because at home we spoke Irish.

DONNCHA: Did you get any experience of drama at school?

SIOBHÁN: Well, I was thrown out of a play in Galway in the Dominicans for giggling. A friend of mine, she had - I can't remember the line but the word 'heart' came into it. The teacher said, 'Now don't say "hart" [with a flat Galway 'a'] say "hawrt".' Of course on the night Helen said 'haart' and I had to say, 'Love is all powerful so do not fear . . .' And of course my whole voice trembled when she said 'haart' and all of the girls then started to giggle. So I was thrown out and I was told I would never be in any more of their plays.

Later I was sent to the St Louis' in Monaghan, and for some strange reason the Louis nuns threw me into the plays, I don't know why. I did such things as *Charley's Aunt* and a lot of others - in translation of course, all in Irish. St Louis' then was an all-Irish school.

Then I used to go to my grandmother's in Longford and that was another facet of Ireland which was full of folklore and stories of ghosts. Then there were all the wonderful summers in the gaeltacht, in the Aran Islands and Carraroe and sometimes Baile an Fheirtéirigh.

DONNCHA: These were the beginnings then of your acting career. Were you formulating ambitions to go on the stage then?

SIOBHÁN: None at all. It was all a game and that's the way it should have remained! No, it was all a game and in Galway there was this old barn owned by the McNallys - they were building contractors. They had this old barn and, talk of barnstorming, that's really where I started. I suppose some of the children didn't want to act and they were in the audience. My sister Nancy always played the heroine. Those plays were in English. We'd make them up as went along. I'd say, This is the story. And of course there was always the villain and I was always the villain. We got moustaches from old mattresses and used our paintboxes from school.

*   *   *

DONNCHA: Can you pick out any single moment where it dawned on you that you might go on the stage?

SIOBHÁN: I think it was Liam O Briain, my French professor, who picked it for me. When I went to Galway University I had no intention of joining the Taibhdhearc, although the Taibhdhearc to me was a place of magic from the age of five. It had wonderful old green curtains and macLiammóir's golden snakes, and they also had a little orchestra in those days and I used to wait with great anticipation for the play which was once a month with people like Proinnsias MacDiarmada, Frank McDermody, who was then an actor. I always remember him playing this maid with a red wig. He was a wonderful actor. And of course we saw Anew McMaster.

No, I hadn't really thought about going on stage. I was always allowed go to the theatre but not to the pictures as we used to call them - that was frowned on. But I was allowed go to the theatre all the time as my father and mother were great theatre-goers.

Walter Macken, then in the Taibhdhearc, tried to inveigle me into taking a part. He told me about a play called *Mary Rose* by J.M. Barrie and I read it and I said: 'But Wally, as soon as I got up on the stage in school people just fell about laughing. They won't take me seriously.' He said, 'You're born to play this.' He had had me in a pageant before this that he had written about St Patrick. He said that I died beautifully when I was baptised, you know, as one of the princesses. Whereas the other princess just went 'boing'! 'Well,' I said, 'it's a matter of interpretation whether you should drop dead or whether you should die gracefully.' Then I said I would translate *Mary Rose* for him but that I couldn't play it and I translated it with the help of Máire Ní Ghiolla Mháirtín who was a wonderful housekeeper we had with the most beautiful Irish. But he somehow persuaded me to play Máire Rós.

Then I played Bessie Burgess, in Irish, and in Eugene O'Neill translations. Even Lady Macbeth! I have a photograph of myself with a very round face and two long thick plaits at the age of eighteen playing Lady Macbeth. We packed the house because I spread the rumour that Eamon de Valera was coming to town and that he was going to come to the play. I didn't tell a lie - I expected him to come, but he didn't. But the audience were swinging out of the rafters and it was very, very successful.

At that time also I used to go around to all the schools and ask for the principal. 'Tá iníon an t-Ollamh MacCionnaith anseo chun é a fheiceáil,' I would say. And of course he would come because my father was not only a university professor but also Supervisor of Exams. So they all wanted to keep in with my father and then I would lecture them that the boys should be sent to the Taibhdhearc instead of to the cinema.

DONNCHA: You were a formidable young woman?

SIOBHÁN: Formidable, yes, and I also got myself on all the committees so that by the time I left Galway all the formal dances were céilís except for the medicals and of course nobody could convert the medicals, at that time anyway. There was a great, great Irish movement in the university at that time.

DONNCHA: You were a crusader, were you?

SIOBHÁN: I was a crusader, yes, and really that's why I went into the Taibhdhearc and that was why my father allowed me do anything in the Taibhdhearc. He thought of it as the language and he never suspected that while I was working for the language I might eventually, much against his wishes, go on the stage.

* * *

DONNCHA: Eventually, you did go on stage. How did it come about?

SIOBHÁN: Well, in my third year at university Wally Macken said: 'Look, Siobhán, what's the point in university? I think you could be a wonderful actress.' And I said, 'Oh don't be silly Wally,' as I intended to go back to Monaghan to become a nun. And I really was determined to do well in my degree for my father's sake. You see, he really was an academic.

And then Liam O Briain, my French professor, did a translation of *Route Nationale Six,* which he called *An Bóthar Mór,* and he told me this day after lectures, he said, 'Each time I'm translating this – he was doing it for Earnán de Blaghad and the Abbey – you just come off the page to me.'

Then in the last term Mr Blythe said that he would like me to play the part. I said to Liam, 'What about studies?' He said it would mean taking about six weeks off. And I said, 'Well, will you still give me first class honours?' And he said, 'No, ní fhéadfainn é sin a dhéanamh; dara grád, dara grád.' That would have broken my father's heart, so I didn't go up to the Abbey and I did get my first honours in French, English and Irish. My father always said, 'Get your bit of paper and you can do as you like then.' And it may sound unimaginative but I was very grateful to him afterwards because it made me very independent.

When I did my first audition for Earnán de Blaghad it was absolutely ridiculous. I mean, Dermot Kelly and my husband Denis O'Dea, they all remembered and it was absolutely awful. We chose to do a piece of *Máire Rós*, but in the scene I chose Máire Rós only had sea and ní hea, and it was the son who had all the big speeches. I started off and I said, 'Where's my fellow actor?' I was told, 'Ah, caithfidh tú é a shamhlú.' I was supposed to imagine him and sit on his knee! So I got myself a chair and I was sitting in mid-air because my son was, sort of, underneath, which made my knees very, very wobbly indeed. Then I had this long speech that I didn't say, you see my son said it and I said sea, then another long speech and I said sea, then another and I said ní hea. And I couldn't remember his next speech and I said, 'Gabh mo leith scéal, caithfidh mé breathnú ar an téacs.' So I went up and looked at the script, came back, another long silence, you know, while my son spoke and then another sea. That finished Blythe. 'Siobhán!' he shouted, 'ná fuil aon spake fada agat?' So then I burst forth into Lady Macbeth! Seemingly the cast had broken from rehearsals and they were all gathered around. Dermot Kelly said people were absolutely fascinated at the mad girl from Galway - that's what they called me - and when I had finished Blythe said, 'Can you type?' I said: 'Certainly not! I only came here for the experience. I'm actually at the university.' And I just marched off and went back to the university.

*   *   *

DONNCHA: How did you finally get into the Abbey?
SIOBHÁN: I was in my digs in Northbrook Road one night when Earnán himself came to me and said that Eithne Dunne was ill, her voice had gone and I was to go down at once and look at the moves and then stay up that night and learn the part. Eithne was a leading actress in a leading role. I wasn't under contract. The last communication I had with Blythe was 'Can you type?' I went down, watched Eithne's moves, rang my cousin, May McKernan, who was in the civil service at the time, asked her if she could come over, sleep in my bed while I learn this and then hear me in the morning. She did. She had to prompt me about four times and then I went down to rehearse with the actors at the theatre and when I had finished I was told that Eithne Dunne had recovered! I did the same thing again for Joan Plunkett and I got into her costume! I got that far!

Then came *Le Bourgeois Gentilhomme* and Liam O Briain said, 'I will have no one but Siobhán playing the little maid,' and that was my first Abbey part. It was an amazing experience because one had to practise laughter. The funny thing is - I was very shy of doing things in front of people except my mother. My mother used to say strange things when I'd be rehearsing for the Taibhdhearc. Rehearsing Lady Macbeth, and she was reading or knitting or sewing and she'd suddenly look up and say: 'I prefer the way you did it before. It was much more sinister when you kept your eyes down when you were talking about Macduff.' She was the only one I liked to rehearse in front of.

Laughter is a very difficult thing to pretend and unfortunately I didn't think *Le Gentilhomme* was all that funny. So this made it even worse. Frank Dermody was directing and he said, 'You'll have to make it spontaneous.' 'It's so difficult,' I said. 'I am not amused.' This was where my university learning came to my help. I said, 'I must go and look at it in the original French.' In those days you were given a script with only your cue at the top and then your own speech.

DONNCHA: You mean, the whole meaning could be missed?

SIOBHÁN: Sometimes you'd actually get your cue at the top of the speech and not at the end. I went home. I was a great reader still - I used to read until two or three in the morning - and I had my copy of *Le Gentilhomme* with me. I saw that Molière had written out, musically, five ha, ha, ha's, seven he, he, he's, three ho, ho, ho's! He had actually written out how many of each! I thought, that is the secret. He being an actor himself, knew how difficult it was, so he had obviously worked it out.

The thing was, when to rehearse? I had to wait until three o'clock in the morning until everyone had gone to bed. I had a room, a little flatlet, and across the corridor was this lovely little lady, very fragile and rather old. Mrs Delahunty owned the house. Well, every night at three o'clock I would start ha, ha, ha-ing and ho, ho, ho-ing and finally there was a knock at my door and there was Mrs Delahunty and the little old lady

The box office at the Old Abbey.

and my face fell because in those days theatrical people had
some extraordinary, awful reputations. Nobody wanted us. I
mean we were still rogues and vagabonds. 'I'm terribly sorry,'
she said, 'Miss . . . has been terribly worried. On the stroke of
three she hears strange noises emanating from the room.'
'Mrs Delahunty,' I said, 'I am a student and I sometimes do
some acting in the Abbey.' Her reaction was: 'Oh,' she said,
'maybe, then, we'll give you a big room downstairs.' And she
gave me this beautiful room downstairs for fifteen shillings
and said was the fifteen shillings too much!

*   *   *

DONNCHA: What was your impression of the Abbey in those
early days?
SIOBHÁN: Oh, I was very impressed because of course I knew
the actors from being a member of the audience. We used to
come up to Dublin specially to the Abbey and indeed to see
Hilton and Micheál. My father would drive me up to see the
theatre - he must have been always interested and he was an
awful fool not to see that he was encouraging me.
F. J. McCormack was there and his wife Eileen Crowe, Mick
Dolan, Maureen Delaney, Eithne Dunne whom I thought was
a superb actress, Bríd Ní Loinsigh, May Craig, Fred Johnson;
Sheila Richards wasn't there, she had gone. There was an
extraordinary company. Then the young ones were Máire Ní
Dhonaill and Micheál O Briain, and I was already there.
DONNCHA: Was the atmosphere of Yeats and Lady Gregory
still around?
SIOBHÁN: It was still around. Of course Denis O'Dea and
Cyril Cusack were there. Denis knew Yeats and Lady
Gregory. There was the old Green Room; one didn't go in
there. I'm sure they wouldn't have minded, but you would
sort of peep in and you would see them in these chintz chairs
reading or knitting and Lady Gregory's portrait over the
mantelpiece where Denis O'Dea always put a bowl of

shamrock every Patrick's Day. And there were wonderful pictures all around.

DONNCHA: There was a spirit, an atmosphere?

SIOBHÁN: There was an amazing atmosphere and one respected it enormously. I always remember the first time Mick Dolan called me Siobhán instead of Miss McKenna. If you gave me a hundred pounds I couldn't have been more elated. I knew I was then accepted.

DONNCHA: It took quite some time before that happened?

SIOBHÁN: Oh, yes! Miss Crowe, Miss Craig, Mr Dolan, Mr McCormack - and in a way that was good for us.

DONNCHA: What about the spirit and the person of Blythe himself?

SIOBHÁN: Blythe! The extraordinary thing is there are more stories told about Blythe than about W. B. Yeats! I mean some of them are hysterical! One didn't always agree with him but the funny thing is that you could have a row with him and he never held it against you, at least he never did with me. I remember him stopping me in full flight in the middle of a dress rehearsal, and I used to go in full flight in a dress rehearsal because I felt this was the most important thing - if I pleased Frank Dermody then, anyone else could have me after that; I just wanted to get it right, get a certain rhythm. I was in the middle of some great speech in an Irish play and Blythe stopped me. 'Ah! d'fhág tú amach séamhú.' And I stood, frozen! And I was so mad I thought the worst thing I can do now is to speak to him in English in the middle of an Irish play. And I said I disagreed but I said, as loud as you like: 'Never do a thing like that to me, stop me in full flight. I mean, have you any understanding or sensitivity? By all means take notes, correct me afterwards.' And everyone was shivering - God! That's the end of her! But he never did.

DONNCHA: You must have been very young, then, when you stood up to him?

SIOBHÁN: Well, I was about twenty. It was not a question of impertinence, it was sheer honesty and emotion and I was mortally wounded that he should stop me then because I was in another world and to hear this voice, 'Ah! Séamhú!'

* * *

DONNCHA: At this stage now, a young girl of twenty, you are beginning to make your way in the Abbey. What ambitions had you?

SIOBHÁN: None. I never remember having ambitions. I was in my first year there and I was asked to do a film called *The Dark Stranger*. F. J. McCormack was to play the father. So I went to F. J. and I said, 'Oh! isn't it wonderful!' I mean one got excited in a childlike way - one was going to be in films! That was the reaction. And he said, 'Oh, I'm not going to be in it.' 'Why?' I asked. 'Oh,' he said, 'I shall never lend my name to anything stage-Irish!' I said, 'Is my part?' He said, 'No, yours isn't, but mine is.' It was the leading role! Then he said to me:'Siobhán, I've no doubt you could be an overnight star on the screen. But I also think you could be a real actress. If you stay with me,' he said, 'with me. If you stay with me in a few years I will make sure.'

So I turned it down and Eileen Crowe, F. J.'s wife, was furious with him. 'He's trying to make you as bad as himself,' she said. Because he used to get offers, but he was totally loyal to the Abbey.

DONNCHA: Is there a certain vanity in greatness? - and he had greatness.

SIOBHÁN: I don't think he was vain at all. He just knew about acting and he knew there was a lot he could teach me. The awful thing was that the next year I went through an awful nine months. Nine months without getting a part having turned down the other one. Most depressing for an actor. I mean it's like any job. If you aren't working it's depressing. And people don't believe this.

Then I was cast as Marion in *The Far-off Hills*. But every time it was about to go on it was cancelled. Eventually, I suppose because of my bit of paper, I wrote to Earnán and said that it was really too much. Also, you see, they had offered me a contract of four pounds a week which sounded wonderful. But when you weren't working it was two pounds and that was starvation. My mother used to send me fresh eggs from Galway because they were fresh, but she didn't know she was sending me my daily meal. And my father was very upset when he read this many years later. I would never have asked him because I had made my decision. It was at that time I was given money for books and I would get the books in the library instead and buy a good meal.

Seán McClory was there at the time, I remember, and I brought some clothes to the pawn and they wouldn't have them because they were light clothes. I remember Seán taking off this big tweed coat and saying, 'Right, and what will you give for that?' And I said, 'Seán! it's winter!' 'Never mind,' he said. And we got about thirty shillings or something and what did we do? We just blew it! We had a good meal, went to the pictures. And I think I had fifteen shillings left for my digs.

But I did resign. I wrote in to Earnán. He rang me up. 'No,' I said. I had given it a lot of thought and I was going off with, of all people, Clopet York. But they were offering me ten pounds a week and I was really tired of the starvation. I also felt it would be very good experience. He sent Denis O'Dea up to my digs and I think he chose Denis because Denis was very good with all the other people. He was terribly kind and I discovered that he had been paying my Equity, one shilling a week, and that infuriated me too as it was up to me whether I became a member of Equity or not. Anyway, he came up and asked me to come and talk to Blythe. And I said, 'Oh, I'm sure that he'll tell me that he has me down for a whole lot of parts, but it's too late.' I went down and he said, 'I have you down for *A Village Wooing* and *The Far-off Hills.*' I said, 'Don't mention *The Far-off Hills!*' But I changed my mind again.

*   *   *

DONNCHA: Was Denis important to your career at that stage?
SIOBHÁN: Well, I didn't know Denis anymore than I knew the

others. I had enormous respect for him. For instance, I remember going into the theatre one day and Denis O'Dea was up on the stage and he was swinging his leg back and forth over the top of a chair. And I thought how odd, and I sat there and couldn't believe it, it went on and on for half an hour. We were allowed go to the theatre one night we wished, we had a free ticket, and I suddenly saw that he had to do this business in the middle of a speech and it had to be slick. That's the kind of rehearsal all of these people used to do and I used to sit in the stalls watching McCormack, Denis, all of them.

* * *

DONNCHA: When would you say did you, as a young actress, get your first break?

SIOBHÁN: Now, what do you mean by break?

DONNCHA: That's a good question. The first big part which brought you to the notice, say, of the public?

SIOBHÁN: Well, *Le Bourgeois Gentilhomme,* the first thing I did and then, *The End House.* I used to read the reviews in those days because one was very innocent and they didn't upset you one way or the other. But I do remember that they were extraordinary and it used to upset me that they put me in front of F. J. McCormack. I mean that they talked about me before the others. Because I really revered McCormack and all of those players and I was right.

DONNCHA: Where would Micheál macLiammóir fit in?

SIOBHÁN: MacLiammóir was a great artist. You see, I used to come up from Galway not only to see the Abbey but also the Longford Players. Then, when I was at the Abbey, I used to go to see the 'leg shows' in the Queens and Jimmy O'Dea. I mean I had very very catholic tastes and learned from all of them.

MacLiammóir and Hilton did wonderful plays in those days, European classics. I always went to the Gate matinées. Some actors aren't great theatre-goers but I always was and still am. I can completely forget where I am if it is good. Bríd Ní Loinsigh and myself went to see a French play. It was *The*

Comedie Française which came to the Gate - their acting is so stylised. We used to do naughty things sometimes on the stage - that night I did a little bit of *Comedie Française*-style acting and Bríd nearly killed me, she actually wanted me to leave the stage. There used to be all kinds of practical jokes, like when I had to smoke this cigarette with this long cigarette holder and you'd come off and suddenly it would blow up. Dermot Kelly would have put a little . . . The things they used to get up to! But it was up to you to carry it off. That was the test.

You were saying when did I get this break. Well, I'll tell you when I got my first slap in the face. I was so accustomed to getting good reviews, really good reviews for everything. I did *Marks and Mabel* and I had all this money, a hundred pounds, to get into a purse - the scene was with Denis O'Dea. After the dress rehearsal I remember Frank Dermody saying; 'That doesn't look like a hundred pounds, will you do something about that' to the prop people. Now, the prop people never consulted me, so on the first night when I opened the rubber band they had padded it out with little balls! I got such a shock that all the money scattered all over the stage and I spent Act I picking it up and Denis O'Dea very kindly picked it up with me, although it was out of character for him to do it. And I had all this Cockney dialogue to do while picking up this money. I was shaking! And during the interval McCormack said, 'Now Siobhán, forget!' But I was crying. 'Just go out there and play the rest of it . . .' and I did. I recovered.

But next day, 'Amateur!' And I thought, how could they say that when they had said I was wonderful? Of course all the actors were up in arms and said it was dreadful. Anyway, it was one of the first long runs the Abbey had. It ran and ran and every afternoon at four o'clock I'd break out into a sweat and run down to the theatre. I had Denis O'Dea out of his mind. I'd say, 'May I look at my prop?', because he had it in his pocket. I would go to the prop man, 'May I see that prop?' But it taught me a lesson. If you have anything to do with a prop, you must check it.

DONNCHA: Small detail?

SIOBHÁN: Then I thought, I'm never going to read the critics again!

DONNCHA: How have you felt about critics over the years?

SIOBHÁN: Well, we need critics because they are part of us. I just feel that some of them really know the theatre and some of them don't know it. But on that occasion a youth came up to my dressing room the next night. I said, 'What are you doing here?' And he said, 'I wanted to see what you thought of my review. I don't usually cover plays. I usually review hurling matches.' I said, 'Get out of my dressing room!'

*　　*　　*

DONNCHA: Siobhán, I suppose a time came when you felt you had to leave the Abbey, you had to change.

SIOBHÁN: It was accidental. In some ways I never left the Abbey. Sheila Richards put me up for a very small part in the film *Hungry Hill*. I could do it in the summer holidays. I think at that time Denis had asked me to marry him. He was offered a part in *Odd Man Out* - funny enough he didn't want to play it and I said, 'Denis, you must play it, it's wonderful.' He said, 'I don't want to play a policeman.' But I said, 'This is some policeman, it is a tremendous script.' So, he went over to do *Odd Man Out* and McCormack, for once, did not think it was stage-Irish and of course he played the wonderful birdman. It was like a family, a little exodus going from the Abbey - we all went off for the month of June to do these films. Then I married Denis in July and later that year Sheila Richards asked me to do *The Playboy of the Western World* at the Edinburgh Festival. The Abbey had been invited and Blythe wouldn't let them go. He was always afraid of letting them go in case, as had happened to such players as Barry Fitzgerald, they all stayed on in Hollywood.

Anyway, Sheila Richards and Lennox Robinson decided they would do *The Playboy*. I had always wanted to do Pegeen Mike. So we went to Edinburgh. We wanted to go as the ex-Abbey Players but Blythe said he would sue us.

Siobhán McKenna with Cyril Cusack in Cherry Orchard.

Then the reviews came out for *Hungry Hill* and although I had only a tiny part I got extraordinary reviews even though I really have to admit I didn't even know where the camera was. And at that time I was offered something like five different Hollywood contracts, from all the big companies. I didn't want to leave Ireland. I didn't want to leave my father and mother. Denis was quite keen because he was also offered contracts. They wanted to groom me as a star. But I heard all kinds of extraordinary stories – that they cut bits off your nose and your behind! So I didn't go.

Then I was offered another film. Blythe did say when we came back after that film, 'I want you to know that you can come back any time.' Now that was very exceptional because generally if you left he didn't want you back. He said it must be one thing or the other. And I understood that because you have to keep a company together.

I did films and plays in London. I did *Eloise and Abelard,* then *St Joan* here in Dublin. I came back, I always came back. I did a season with Cyril, touring with *The Playboy* and *Arms and the Man.* Then a season with Hilton and Micheál, which was my first with them. That was very enjoyable. Hilton was always very imaginative about me. Some people are inclined to put me in tragedy. Hilton said a lovely thing to me. He rushed up to me at rehearsals one day and said, 'It's like driving a Rolls Royce. I'm tired of my Baby Ford!' He was very good with me.

DONNCHA: Was it the St Joan part that brought you to fame internationally?

SIOBHÁN: I remember somebody saying it was the first time they saw reviews on the front page. In a way, she has dogged me because people keep saying, Oh, St Joan! And I would say, Look, I have done just as good work.

In America I made *Life* magazine about four or five times. So also did Marilyn Monroe but for very different reasons! I met Marilyn.

DONNCHA: Did you form any impression of her?

SIOBHÁN: Yes, I loved her. She was terribly innocent and truly had a sweet expression. She came with her then husband, Arthur Miller, and I have a photograph of us somewhere, which amuses people - when the photographer came in I kept on speaking so I'm in profile, but Marilyn - it's the training - immediately Marilyn reacted. Later when I met her she had changed her hair, and I said 'Marilyn, you've cut your hair!' And she turned to Arthur Miller and said, 'Did you hear that? She noticed that I cut my hair!' There was a great insecurity in her.

DONNCHA: Innocence?

SIOBHÁN: Innocence and insecurity and a great sweetness.

DONNCHA: The American experience is one that you cherish.

SIOBHÁN: I do.

* * *

DONNCHA: What is it that makes an actor great?

SIOBHÁN: There has to be something there first of all - hard work and experience improves it. McCormack had that and a lot of the Abbey people had it. I think Niall Buggy has it. MacLiammóir had it. Hilton was a better actor than Micheál, but Micheál had this something else - na súile. He did it with the eyes.

DONNCHA: Then you found yourself, as Micheál did too, in the world of the one-person show. Did that appeal to you as a medium?

SIOBHÁN: It is a difficult medium. MacLiammóir adored it. It depends on my audience. Certain audiences I enjoyed. In America and Australia I enjoyed it. You know you are bringing them something. But here it is a little bit like bringing coals to Newcastle. What happens is your authors, and in a way your audience, become your fellow actors. I do prefer to have my fellow actors, although Micheál said: 'Don't you love doing the one-person show? At least I give myself the cue properly!'

* * *

DONNCHA: I see a picture of Eamon de Valera over your fireplace there. What memories have you of him?

SIOBHÁN: I always loved Dev. Now that I've grown up, I don't think I agree with everything. As a child I just absolutely loved him. He had charisma. I know some people hated him but he had a bigness about him. He was larger than life.

DONNCHA: He was pre-microphone.

SIOBHÁN: He certainly was and this is very important. He was an orator as well. He told me he was on the Abbey stage one time. A friend of his was producing a play, an amateur play, and an actor fell ill and they asked Dev to take over. So Dev said, 'I've never been on the stage!' But his friend said: 'Listen, you'll do. Anyone can do it, he's playing a doctor.'

He went in for the rehearsal and was told, 'You'll have to project!' Anyway, he didn't get another rehearsal, so that night he went on and said in a very loud voice, 'Bhfuil tú go maith?' - projecting. And the director told him he would make a great orator, that he could be heard down at Nelson's Pillar!

Biography

Siobhán McKenna was born in Belfast on 24 May 1923. When she was about five, her father was appointed Professor of Mathematics in University College Galway, and the family moved to Galway. Siobhán studied French, Irish and English at the University in Galway and acted in the Taibhdhearc. She then went on to write a thesis on the French theatre for her M.A., and joined the Abbey Theatre. There she met Denis O'Dea, one of the leading young actors of the time, and they were married in 1946.

She and her husband enjoyed great success on both stage and screen. In 1956 they starred in separate Broadway shows at the same time. Two parts in which Siobhán won special acclaim were St Joan in G. B. Shaw's play and Pegeen Mike in Synge's *Playboy of the Western World*. In 1958 the *Evening*

Standard named her the best actress of the year. She has appeared in eight films, including the very successful *Dr. Zhivago*.

In the spring of 1970, she presented her one-woman show *Here Are Ladies* in London and later took it to the United States. The ladies she featured were taken from the plays of G. B. Shaw, J. M. Synge and Sean O'Casey. James Joyce was represented by Molly Bloom in her famous soliloquy. Everywhere she played to packed houses.

Siobhán McKenna has received many signal honours, at home and abroad. In January 1975, the then President, Cearbhall Ó Dálaigh, appointed her to the Council of State, which the President convenes from time to time to aid and counsel him on all matters on which he may consult it. She is the only woman member. In April 1971 the Eire Society of Boston awarded her their Gold Medal, for her public service to the arts. Previous distinguished recipients of this medal included John F. Kennedy, Cardinal Cushing, John Ford and John Huston, and Cornelius Ryan, author of the best-selling *The Longest Day*.

In December 1971 the University of Dublin, Trinity College, made her an honorary Doctor of Literature. And in June 1983, the Royal Dublin Society made her a life member in recognition of the excellence of her theatrical art and her dedication in achieving internationally renowned performances.

Her husband, Denis O'Dea, died in Dublin on 5 November 1978 at the age of seventy five. Their only child, Donncha, is a former Irish swimming champion and noted poker player.

Few Irish actresses before her have had her educational background, which gave her fluency in Irish and French and a knowledge of the literary heritage in both these languages and particularly of the French theatre.

Great actresses and little theatres are seldom allied, but Siobhán McKenna, as her talk with Donncha O Dúlaing shows, has remained a good friend of Galway's Taibhdhearc.

Mick Mackey

The first hurler I ever heard of was Mick Mackey. His was the name, loved by Limerick and feared and respected by all others in the days of my early boyhood in Doneraile.

All of us who as children hurled imaginary All-Irelands in our back gardens created our own mythology. A good goalkeeper became Paddy Scanlan, a back was always Batt Thornhill, the only barber in Buttevant, and a forward was always Mick Mackey.

We learned those particular names when Hitler was just about to launch World War II, when the only news was contained in the *Cork Examiner,* and when Doneraile's only contact with the outside world was the Newcastle West bus which called morning and evening. How we learned them is still a mystery to me. Perhaps we discovered through listening to the 'boys' who would gather for hurling talk and pitch-and-toss in the long summer evenings of 1939 and 1940.

Anyway, Mick Mackey was our hero and many a youngster saw himself as the great man from Ahane.

It was much later that I saw Mick Mackey in person. I can still remember the ripple of excitement as Ahane took the field in a tournament game in Charleville in the mid-forties. Old men cheered and waved caps as the magic words 'Up Ahane' and 'Come on Mick Mackey' told us youngsters that mythology had become reality. Mick was, of course, far beyond his prime, yet I have a vivid memory of a twenty-one-yards free and the ball leaping like a wild thing in the back of a startled net. The magic of Mackey was not quite gone.

Then, as happens all great players, he faded from our young minds. Other players, other teams, other games assumed their own importance. It seemed that Mick Mackey was gone. But, in the mid-fifties he returned, returned to train a splendid young hurling team they christened 'Mackey's Greyhounds'. A more rotund Mick took his place in the limelight and, but for the might of Wexford, might have re-kindled the Limerick hurling flame.

Years passed and Ann Mulqueen, the great ballad-singer from Castleconnell, and, of course, an avid Mackey and Ahane supporter, urged me to bring 'Highways and Byways' to the village. I did. A night of storytelling, singing and anecdote unparalleled reached into the small hours. Séan Herbert, John Mackey, Mick Hickey, Willie Keane and his late father, Jack, a founder of Ahane, and others opened the floodgates of memory. But where was Mick Mackey? Some said 'Mick will talk to no one.' Others, helpfully said, 'Sure, Mick did all his hurling and talking on the field.' Was the great man ever to be captured? Were his memories as elusive as the flying ball of his solo-running days?

And then, in 1979, that splendid GAA Club, Na Piarsaigh invited me to Caherdavin in Limerick to present medals to their young heroes of that year. I was delighted. There I met Séamus Ó Ceallaigh, the doyen of Limerick GAA historians, who whispered conspiratorially into my ear, 'He's outside. Mick is here. He'd like to meet you.' I was stunned. And Mick Mackey was there. He sat quietly and modestly in a corner. Without preamble he said quietly, as if we were continuing a conversation, 'I'm sorry I missed you that night in Castle-connell. My wife Kitty says if you're ever passing Ard-nacrusha, drop in to see us.' I didn't know what to say. 'What can I do for you?' he asked, and then added, like the humble man he was, 'Maybe what I have to say wouldn't interest you!' I switched on the tape-recorder.

MICK: It was my grandfather who first gave me a hurley. He used to cut hurleys and have them made up. There were always hurleys at home, because my father also hurled.

DONNCHA: Were there many in your family?

MICK: There were ten, although two died young. It was always hurling and talking about hurling in our house. There was a little paddock at the back where we used to have a few pucks now and then. The field was owned by local gentry and often you might be only ten minutes there when you'd have to run for it. We had only to get over the wall and we were back in our own place.

DONNCHA: Hurling was always a topic of conversation.

MICK: It was. 'Twas always talked about. My father would be going back to the years when he was hurling. My grandfather hurled too, of course, and was captain of the Castleconnell team in those days, way back in the eighteen eighties at the time of the foundation of the GAA.

'Twasn't easy to get my father to talk. He might though, if you were on your own with him, especially in the fields, for example, making hay. We had hay ourselves and he might open up, but otherwise, he wasn't a talkative man.

DONNCHA: The hurleys you used were made locally?

MICK: There was a carpenter married to an aunt of mine. He was the man who made them. You might be asking him to make one for a month, running up and down to his house, doing messages for him, trying to please him! And then, eventually, one day when you arrived he'd have your hurley made. He'd have it behind the door and as you ran in he'd hand it out. O'Connor was his name.

DONNCHA: Did you have a sliotar [special ball] in those days?

MICK: Oh no. Sometimes we had a sponge ball. It was very seldom that you'd have a sliotar because we couldn't afford one.

But I remember the 1923 Limerick team training for the All-Ireland - the game wasn't played until 1924. There were two All-Irelands played in the same year. It was up in Keane's

Mick Mackey.

field that they trained. I would stand at one end of the puck-around and my brother John would stand at the other and we'd return the ball to them every time it came our way. They had goal-posts laid down and we actually pucked the real sliotar.

* * *

DONNCHA: When did you first play for an actual team?
MICK: 1928. I played with the Ahane junior team in 1928.
DONNCHA: In what position?
MICK: Right-half-forward. We won the championship. That was the first championship that Ahane won. It wasn't played until 1929. The final was played in Adare against Feenagh-Kilmeedy. We had a great following. We always took three or four buses. That was the beginning for Ahane. We had to play intermediate hurling the next year and we went senior in 1930.
DONNCHA: When did you first play on a Limerick team?
MICK: I was a sub in 1929 against Cork in the League. I made the Limerick junior team in 1930 and we drew with Tipperary in Clonmel. We came back here to Limerick for the re-play and they beat us - Tipp. won three All-Irelands that year, minor, junior and senior.
DONNCHA: Even with all that and Cork's victory in 1931, Limerick were really about to come into their own.
MICK: They were, and even in 1931, they gave Tipperary a good match in the Championship, in Cork. I really came on the senior team in 1932.
DONNCHA: That must have been a good year for you.
MICK: Well, '32 was fairly good. We were beaten by Cork. We were somewhat unlucky and fairly green. We had a few great veterans, but most of us were too young, too green. However, the next year we were a different team. We weren't green anymore. We got to the final against Kilkenny.

Then we had a great run, a terrific run. We improved and we went into the final again the next year, in 1934, when we played a draw with a fine Dublin team. We played the replay very late in October. We beat them. It was very tight. My brother John played on my right. Timmy Ryan was the captain. By the way, Jim Barry of Cork trained us for the replay. We beat Dublin 5-2 to 2-6. It was one of the greatest days in my life.

We swept through Munster in 1935. There was no one to hold us. But the final - well bad weather and a single point by Kilkenny beat us that day.

We went to America in 1936 in the month of May and everyone said, When they come back, they'll beat no one! We came and nothing could stop us! As a matter of fact I believe that the 1936 men were as good a team as ever wore the green and white of Limerick.

DONNCHA: Which of the players do you remember?

MICK: All of them. I was privileged to be captain and to be with the greatest bunch of hurlers that ever went out from any county. Every one of them was a star, from the goalie to the left-full-forward. If I had a bad day, the fellow longside me was twice as good. That was how it worked. There was a tremendous comradeship. There was a great spirit and they were all strong fellows. There was no codding about them!

DONNCHA: They were hard hurlers?

MICK: They could play it any way you liked. If you wanted it nice, they could be nice, but, I'll tell you, they could be ruthless too. No one could mess that Limerick team around. They were a great team. 'Tis hard to name them all, but I love them all, I remember them. *(At this, Mick paused and there were tears in his eyes as he struggled with memory and emotion.)* You could say that in all the positions we had stars.

We gave Kilkenny a bad beating, really. Some said 'twas a bad All-Ireland, but not for us! No one could live with us that day. I'll never forget that team.

*   *   *

DONNCHA: When you look back over all the years, which, Mick, was your greatest game?

MICK: I think the best match I played was in Thurles in 1935 against Cork. Clohessy had been sent to the line after fifteen minutes and we had only fourteen men when we beat them. That was my best individually. As we were a man short, I played like two men between centre-field and centre-forward.

DONNCHA: Did you have any special training methods?

MICK: No. But we had a great trainer called Peter Brown. He was a great physical man. We trained very hard.

DONNCHA: People always talk about you and your skill as a solo runner. Was this a style, a skill, that you cultivated?

MICK: I suppose they do. It really all began accidentally. I never planned it. It started in a Railway Cup match. Dan Canniffe was centre-half-back for Leinster, and I swerved around him at one stage in the game, saw an opening and started to run with the ball on my hurley. Nowadays they run with the ball resting on the stick, but I always ran hopping it on the hurley, which made it more difficult to control. I ran about thirty yards and when I threw up the ball to hit it, Peter Blanchfield of Kilkenny, who was left-full-back for Leinster, hit it for me! He sent it back up the field. That was my first real solo-run! And 'twas no success!

After that, I got into the habit of it. Whether it was good or bad, I can't say. You see, it was great if you scored, but if you didn't 'twas gone back over your head again and the loose opponent had it. There is no point in going on a solo-run unless you are going to score at the end of it!

DONNCHA: Was there any particular time in a game when you would go on a solo-run?

MICK: Well, you see, if things were going against you, that was the time to break through and score a point after a solo-run. That was a great boost to the rest of the lads.

DONNCHA: I suppose, too, that you were what people called 'a marked man'.

MICK: Oh no, not at all. At that time it was man marking man, very close and very tough. If you weren't good enough or strong enough, you had no business playing the game of hurling. Centre-forward now, where I played, that's a very hard place, the hardest place on the team.

DONNCHA: Why do you say that?

MICK: Well, you see, if you beat the centre-half, the other half-backs would not be too far away. More often than not, the centre-forward has two and maybe three men to cope with. At my time 'twas vital, because say with Scanlan pucking out, he'd drive it well past centre field and every ball would drop in my area. You'd be murdered from him, he was that good! He was so good, God forgive me, you'd pray he'd miss it now and again! But he never did.

*　*　*

DONNCHA: If you had life over again, would you go hurling?

MICK: I would indeed. I look back at all the fine people I've met. I'd have met no one if I hadn't gone hurling. I had four trips to America. I had a great life in hurling. I was lucky. Any of the other lads in our team would have been entitled to as much as I got. They were all stars. I was really only one-fifteenth of a team, like anyone else.

DONNCHA: Which medal do you cherish most?

MICK: The medal I cherish most, I haven't got. It was the 1934 Championship Jubilee Year. It was my first medal and I treasured it, but I gave it away to a great friend of mine in New York.

*　*　*

DONNCHA: I suppose, inevitably, we must talk of other famous players. Did Christy Ring impress you?

MICK: Oh yes. He was fierce dangerous. I played at least four years with him on Railway Cup teams. Jack Lynch, Jim Young, Paddy Donovan, John Quirke and Billy Murphy, I played with all of them. They were fantastic.

But we can't forget the Kilkenny fellows. I remember Peter Reilly and Eddie Doyle in the early days and, of course, the

*Mick Mackey leads the Limerick team onto the field in the
All-Ireland semi-final, 1940.*

great Paddy Phelan. He was an attacking player, who often marked my brother, John. Where would you leave Lory Meagher and Jimmy Walshe of Carrickshock, the 'Yank' Dunne and Mattie Power? They were comrades, great gentlemen. I don't think there was ever a strong word between Kilkenny and ourselves. It was hurling all the time.

The match I most enjoyed was when we beat Kilkenny at the end of April in 1935. It was an exhibition. Never more than two points between us. The score was 2-6 to 2-4 at the end. There were 25,000 spectators at it. You always know you're beaten when the crowd starts to leave - if you're in front you have won, if you're behind, you have lost. No one stirred that day. We were level with minutes to go and I scored a point and John scored another. I was never as glad to hear a final whistle blow. Winning in Kilkenny was it!

Biography

Mick Mackey was born on 12 July 1912 into a well-known Limerick hurling family from Castleconnell. He was one of the outstanding hurlers of the thirties, as shown by his playing record. He won All-Ireland medals in 1934, 1936 and 1940, and was captain of the Limerick team when he won the two last. He won fifteen hurling championships, five Munster championships and eight Railway Cup medals, as well as National League medals. He received the Texaco Hall of Fame award and the Bank of Ireland 'All-time Great' award.

He was noted for his great skill and physical strength. Jack Lynch of Cork said, 'Mick Mackey could go through a stone wall.' A prolific scorer and an inspiring leader, his best position was centre-forward.

He is credited with introducing the solo-run with the ball on the stick. However, an English traveller in Ireland in the seventeenth century, one John Dunton, describing a hurling match, wrote, 'On this broad part (of the stick), you may sometimes see one of the gamesters carry the ball, tossing it forty or fifty yards in spite of all the adverse players; and when he is like to lose it, he generally gives it a great stroke to drive it towards the goal.' It looks, then, as though Mick Mackey, an instinctive hurler, revived a technique which had fallen out of use, rather than introducing something entirely new.

Hurling is acclaimed as the fastest field game in the world. A distinctively Irish sport, it dates back to pre-historic Ireland and the heroic deeds of Cuchulainn who won victory single-handed with his bronze hurley against three fifties of the boy-troops of Ulster.

The colonists took to hurling after the Norman invasion, and in alarm at this yielding to native ways, their overlords banned hurling by the Statutes of Kilkenny in 1366. This edict seems to have had little effect, for it was found necessary to ban the game again by the Statutes of Galway in 1527.

When asked his opinion of the standard of hurling in his later days, Mick Mackey said, 'Hurling is too timid nowadays, and players do not practise enough. In my young days we practised every evening and Sunday morning, but then we had nothing else to do. There are too many distractions today.'

It is not strange that Mick Mackey became such a great hurler, coming as he did from a hurling family and a county steeped in hurling tradition. (Few counties shine at both football and hurling. A Kerry footballer once contemptuously described Kerry hurling as 'compulsory tillage'.) When hurling fans meet, the argument goes on: which was the best player ever, Mick Mackey or Christy Ring, a question difficult to decide as they reached their peak in different decades.

Mick Mackey spent his entire working life with the ESB at Ardnacrusha, first as a driver and then as supervisor, save for the years of World War II, when he served in the army. He became a coach and selector for Limerick after he retired from the playing field. He died on 13 September 1982 at the age of seventy.

Paschal McGuinness

Paschal McGuinness is Vice-President and Business Manager of 'Local Union 608' of the United Brotherhood of Carpenters and Joiners of America. He controls '608' from his office, high above the strident din of Broadway in New York City. He is a slim, quietly-spoken but resolute man who is among the leaders of Irish opinion in the United States.

Paschal is at once patriotic and pragmatic. His allegiances, on the one hand to Ireland and on the other to his family and the United States, are sharply etched on his mind.

He was not unduly enthusiastic about an interview. Would I take a rain-check? I wouldn't. At first, as he sat behind his desk, facing the flag of the United States, a picture of John F. Kennedy and one of St Joseph, the Worker, he was almost monosyllabic. His replies, clipped and truthful, did not invite any 'slack' questions, but, soon, his reluctance vanished and was replaced by a mutual trust. I met two of his Union colleagues over lunch and they, much to his embarrassment, regaled me with tales of Paschal's generosity, his kindness towards the needy, his constantly-extended hand of friendship to youth and, his help, both material and spiritual, to worthy causes.

Paschal McGuinness, the young man from Cootehill who went to the USA in the fifties with a heartful of dreams and pocketless of dollars, is a worthy voice in my voices of Ireland. He combines in himself the best of the land of his birth and the

*Paschal McGuinness talks to Donncha in his office in
New York.*

most generous traits of the country which made him, and others like him, welcome in darker days.

PASCHAL: When I left Ireland in 1957, I left because I couldn't get a job in Dublin. I walked the streets for about three weeks and couldn't find any suitable work in the building and construction trades and then I decided to come to the United States.

DONNCHA: How did you travel?

PASCHAL: I came by boat from Cobh, Co. Cork.

DONNCHA: Can you take us back to your early years?

PASCHAL: My roots are in Cootehill, Co. Cavan. I went to St Michael's Boys' School and I played football for Cootehill in the Cavan County Championship. We won the junior in 1952 and the senior in 1953, '54, '55, and '56. Those were great days!

DONNCHA: What ambitions did you have as a young lad?

PASCHAL: Well at that time I decided to serve my time in the carpentry trade, because it was the only job available and my father, God be merciful to him, knew Mick Mullan who was a carpenter and a cabinet maker in Cootehill and, in that way, I began to serve my time.

DONNCHA: How long did you serve?

PASCHAL: Six years. At that time you had to pay £50 to begin, but we couldn't afford it. My father got me in the backdoor, without paying.

DONNCHA: Did you have a natural aptitude for carpentry or joinery?

PASCHAL: Well I always liked to work with my hands and I was creative and liked to see a finished product.

DONNCHA: Had your family been tradesmen in the past?

PASCHAL: Well, yes. My uncle, Paddy Reilly, was a tradesman in Cootehill, going back fifty years.

DONNCHA: Were you paid anything during the apprenticeship?

PASCHAL: For the first six months there was no pay. After that it was sixteen shillings a week.

DONNCHA: And how much of that were you able to keep for yourself?

PASCHAL: Well, I gave my mother fifteen shillings and I kept one for myself.

DONNCHA: Do you remember what you spent the bob on?

PASCHAL: Well, I suppose the pictures in St Michael's hall, which cost fourpence, three half-pence on some sweets, and, as for the rest, I don't remember!

DONNCHA: So, when you served your time you had to look for a job.

PASCHAL: That's right. After eighteen months I went to work in Monaghan town as an improver. I stayed there for a year and then I went to Dublin.

DONNCHA: You walked the city looking for work?

PASCHAL: Yes. I worked in Drumcondra for a year, but things went sour and I went to Pye Radio in Dundrum and I then went to Jordans in Granby Lane and when I finished that I couldn't find a job, so I decided to emigrate.

DONNCHA: Did you try very hard to get work?

PASCHAL: Yes, I never wanted to emigrate or to leave Ireland.

DONNCHA: When you had to leave, was there a big family consultation?

PASCHAL: Yes. My mother wasn't happy nor was my father. But it was a necessity. There was no work and I had no option but to leave.

DONNCHA: You left from Cobh. How did you travel there?

PASCHAL: We travelled by taxi from Cootehill. It was a friend of ours who drove us down. It was a sad and lonely trip. I think that the memory that will stay in my mind until the day I die is leaving my mother on the gangway when I said goodbye at the boat.

DONNCHA: Departures from Cobh were horrendous at that time.

PASCHAL: I would say that the most accurate way to describe it was that it was like somebody dying. You left Ireland in 1957 and you might never see your family again.

DONNCHA: You were a young lad at that time. Were you aware at all that you were part of the terrible haemorrhaging tradition of Irish emigration?

PASCHAL: Yes, I was aware of it. At that time there was a lot of emigration from Ireland to the United States and it was the only place to go, apart from England. I thought that there were better and more opportunities here than in England.

* * *

DONNCHA: What memory have you of your first sight of New York?

PASCHAL: Well, my first sight was of 55th Street on 12th Avenue at the Cunard Lines where the Mauretania berthed in New York. It wasn't a very pleasant first sight. I was scared. I was nineteen years old and it wasn't a very pleasant feeling.

DONNCHA: Were they very severe in checking out people?

PASCHAL: No, not really. I had all my papers in order.

DONNCHA: Had you much money?

PASCHAL: I had about fourteen dollars in my pocket.

DONNCHA: That didn't leave you much leeway?

PASCHAL: No, it didn't. I had no leeway. I met a friend of mine from Kildare, a Mr O'Toole, who claimed me out here. He brought me to his apartment and I stayed there until I got organised.

DONNCHA: Were you long here before you got work?

PASCHAL: I arrived on a Saturday and I joined the local 608 Union on the Monday and I went to work on the following Wednesday.

DONNCHA: You didn't hang around?

PASCHAL: I didn't. I had a few friends. I met some from the Cavan Football Club in New York on that Saturday evening and they set it up. It was because of friends and people who were here before me that I got work so fast.

DONNCHA: What was your impression of work standards here by comparison with what you had known at home?
PASCHAL: There was no problem. I joined the Union before I started the work.
DONNCHA: Is it an old Union?
PASCHAL: We've just celebrated one hundred years of the Brotherhood of Carpenters and Joiners of America, here in New York. We're one of the oldest unions in the building and construction trades and one of the greatest.
DONNCHA: I wonder what it was like before the Union?
PASCHAL: Well, the reasons behind the founding of it are quite simple: a fair day's pay for a fair day's work. The people who came before us worked for little money and for long hours. The labour movement has ensured that a working man and his family can get a decent day's work and pay his bills at the end of it in reasonable comfort.
DONNCHA: Did you hear stories from older men when you came here about the harder times before they were unionised?
PASCHAL: Yes, a very good friend of mine, John Tierney, was telling me one time that his father and mother both came over from Leitrim and were living in an apartment on the East Side. John tells the story that on one occasion when they were having dinner his mother said, 'John, son, dip your bread in the gravy, leave the meat for your father.' The point is that the good old days are right now. I think this country was never as good as it is now for the average working person.

* * *

DONNCHA: Were you long in the Union before you began to get interested in its workings, its organisation?
PASCHAL: In the beginning I worked as a carpenter, then as a foreman, a superintendent. I really did not get involved in politics in the local union for the first five or six years.
DONNCHA: Was it difficult to break in?
PASCHAL: It wasn't really. I knew a lot of people who were involved in politics in the local union. I attended some meetings and in 1967 I was approached to run as a delegate for

the district Council, which is just a part-time position. I ran and I won.

DONNCHA: When did you first become professionally involved with the Union?

PASCHAL: I first became professionally involved in 1970. At that stage, the full-time Treasurer/Secretary passed away, Jim Neary from Newry. So the job was open. At that time the President of the Local, John O'Connor from Galway City, asked me if I would be interested in running for the position. When I ran I made sure that I would make it. Of course I had opposition the first time. But I won by six or seven hundred votes.

DONNCHA: You're now in a very powerful position?

PASCHAL: I wouldn't say a powerful position. I would rather say that it's a position from which I get a good deal of satisfaction. I can put people to work. I'm in a position to help people and I get great pleasure from that.

DONNCHA: What philosophy do you have about work, about the Union, about people?

PASCHAL: First of all, among the unions, we are a brotherhood. We are there to help those in need. If a man with a family is out of work, it is our job to find work for him at a fair wage, which is as much as any of us can expect from life. We work very closely with the other building trades. We have a Building Trades Council to which all of the unions belong.

DONNCHA: Do you have contact with the 'Bosses'?

PASCHAL: Well, the 'Bosses', as you call them, have a very close working relationship with the unions because we negotiate agreements every three years. We try to settle the best way we can for our membership. We also understand that the contract has to make some money too and, in that way, keep our people working. So, we have a very good Union scale with very good fringe benefits and good protection as far as our members are concerned.

DONNCHA: The Labour Movement in the United States is quite different from Labour as we understand it at home in Ireland.

PASCHAL: Well, really Labour is the same all over the world, but, the difference here is that we are more conservative, that we do sit down and try to straighten out our problems. We do not have many strikes. We preach that to our membership because we feel that a strike is of no use to anyone. If a member is on strike he is not being paid, so nobody gains by it. The Carpenters Union have never had a strike in the last hundred years. We have always had very good negotiating teams. I have sat through negotiations. We have had tough fights and differences of opinion with the contractors, but in the end it was ironed out. The members were satisfied and the contractors were satisfied. Everyone came out on top.

* * *

DONNCHA: You have retained close links with Ireland over the years?

PASCHAL: Yes, very close links. I love to go back to see my mother and brothers and sister.

DONNCHA: And the Irish situation at home, both political and national, interests you?

PASCHAL: Yes, I think every Irishman must be concerned about the problems in Ireland. We in the trade union movement, especially, have formed the American Labour for Irish Freedom, but we would want to see it effected by peaceful means.

DONNCHA: What do you think of Irish attitudes to the problem?

PASCHAL: We found that most of the Irish people would like to see a free Ireland. At the same time, we do feel that in parts of Ireland, people are very unconcerned. The Irish-Americans are often more concerned about the freedom of Ireland than are the people living in Ireland.

DONNCHA: This brings us to an interesting point. I have attended the St Patrick's Day Parade in New York and found it so different from what we have in Ireland - so vivid, so alive, so magnificent. Why is this?

PASCHAL: I would say that when you are away from your homeland that you are more patriotic, more aware of fond memories of Ireland and that is at least one reason why there might be more enthusiasm than there is at home.

DONNCHA: Do you feel that Ireland has often not been sufficiently aware of the work of Irish-Americans and their generosity towards Irish causes, charities and the like?

PASCHAL: Well, let me put that in a different way. I would not say that they are unappreciative of what the average Americans do but that the average American means well but that we, perhaps, do the wrong thing. Also, we often go over there and try to tell them our way of doing things. I think that Ireland should be left to the Irish. Certainly, if we can help in any way to aid the Irish economy to get more jobs, people working over there, even to help towards the complete freedom, we should do so, but behind the scenes. The Irish must lead in Ireland.

*   *   *

DONNCHA: Now I know at home in the old days the American letter was always very important, and the American parcel was even more important; did you send many American letters home in your time?

PASCHAL: I always tried to write as often as possible. As far as the parcel is concerned, I will say this to you, that I arrived in New York city on September 21st 1957, and for Christmas I sent my mother home a hundred dollars, which was a lot of money in '57. I borrowed that hundred dollars.

DONNCHA: Did you write home on a regular basis?

PASCHAL: Yes, I wrote on a monthly basis.

DONNCHA: How important was religion to you?

PASCHAL: I would say very important. That is a very interesting question. I think that my background, the way that we were brought up at home, my mother's teachings to us as regards the Catholic religion, had a big bearing on my life and on my family.

DONNCHA: Was life more difficult for a youngster than now, say, around New York?

PASCHAL: That's a tough question. I think that at that time life was probably just as tough, but we didn't have the drug problem, we didn't have many of the problems you have today at that time. You could use the subways in New York city at twelve o'clock at night or two o'clock in the morning and you wouldn't be afraid of being mugged. So I think that we were safer and probably more innocent at that time than we are today.

DONNCHA: You met your wife in New York?

PASCHAL: I met my wife in New York city, in the Jaegar House on 85th Street on Lexington Avenue.

DONNCHA: What is the Jaegar House?

PASCHAL: Well, the Jaegar House was a very noted Irish dance hall at that time.

DONNCHA: And what did the young Irish people do? Did they go dancing? Was that the main hobby?

PASCHAL: At that time we went every Friday and Saturday night, and I attended most of the Irish dances.

DONNCHA: Where does your wife come from?

PASCHAL: From Ballyhayes, Co. Cavan, which is approximately five miles from Cootehill.

DONNCHA: You didn't travel far from home to meet her?

PASCHAL: Well, I didn't travel very far at all. As a matter of fact, when were over in Cavan last year on vacation, we were travelling from Ballyhayes to Cootehill and my wife said to me, 'I didn't know you lived so close!'

Biography

In the forties and the fifties of the last century more than a million Irish men and women fled to America from famine-stricken Ireland. An American commentator of the time wrote, 'America demands for her development an inexhaustible fund of physical energy, and Ireland supplies the most part of it.' And in 1836 an Irishman in America reflected sadly, 'How often do we see such paragraphs in the paper as "an Irishman drowned" - "an Irishman crushed by a beam" - "an Irishman suffocated in a pit" - "an Irishman blown to atoms by a steam engine" - "twenty Irishmen buried alive by the sinking of a bank" - and other like casualties and perils to which honest Pat is constantly exposed in the hard toils for his daily bread.'

Those bad old days are gone, thanks mainly to Irish pioneers of organised labour. One of the first was the legendary Mother Jones, born in Cork about 1830. She emigrated to America as a child and spent her life fighting for the rights of factory and mill hands, miners and children. She lived to be a hundred and regretted that she had to die before her work was completed. Later came Austin Hogan from county Clare and Michael Quill, the Kerryman, who between them founded the Transport Union of America.

The American Federation of Labor was also largely the creation of the Irish. The largest Union in the Federation at the turn of the century was the Brotherhood of Carpenters, with an Irishman, Peter J. McGuire, as its long-time secretary-treasurer.

The tradition is carried on today by Paschal McGuinness from Cootehill, Co. Cavan, who is Vice-President of Local 608 of the Brotherhood. For this quiet man in his late forties, America has been truly the land of opportunity. He seized his chance, not to make a large fortune, but to carve out a rewarding career. One of the striking points he makes about Trade Unionism in the United States is their reluctance to call a strike, because of their pragmatic realisation that a strike does no good to either side, and least of all to the workers. He sees negotiation as by far the best way of settling any problems in labour-employer relations.

Edna O'Brien

One fine day in the middle of the night, two dead men got up to fight, two blind men looking on, two cripples running for a priest and two dummies shouting Hurry on. That's how it is. Topsy turvy. Lit with blood, cloth wick and old membrane. Milestones, tombstones, whetstones and mirrors. Mirrors are not for seeing by, mirrors are for wondering at, and wondering into. There was a piece of glass by which we tried to catch and contain the sun's fire. It must have been called a sunglass. There is so little and so fucking much. Half a lifetime. Felt, seen, heard, not fully felt, most meagrely seen, scarcely heard at all, and still in me, rattling, like a receding football, or Count Dracula's swagger.

Edna O'Brien read the opening of her novel *Night* for the '3-0-1' radio programme. She laid down her manuscript and leaning towards me, looking straight into my eyes in that direct way of hers, asked, 'Is that enough?' Taking my silence for acquiescence she followed with the closing lines of the same novel, in that strange incantatory style of hers: 'Oh star of the morning, oh slippery path, oh guardian angel of mortals, givvus eyes, lend us a hand, lead us to the higher shores of life, of bolden, lawless, transubstantiating love.'

She seemed lost in the silence that followed, a stillness in which it seemed that she was back again in the pristine world of *The Country Girls*. The question, when posed, seemed unnecessary.

Edna O'Brien.

DONNCHA: Edna, county Clare figures largely in your mind?

EDNA: Oh, utterly. I believe that you come from where you come from, not just in your own mortal life but in your ancestors. I believe fully in what Jung called the collective unconscious, I believe in ancestry and mythology, and it wasn't by accident nor was it a sneer at the Catholic church that made me call one of my novels *A Pagan Place.* I mean, the pagans were there before the Christians and county Clare is an extraordinary county, it is like a kind of ghost. You know, you drive along it and while all of Ireland is beautiful in its manifold kinds of ways, there's something about Clare that is so rivetting and I don't just say that as any sort of nostalgic thing. I find that I see in a way the ordinariness of its extraordinariness. It's not scenic in that sense that you would have postcards made of it. You know there's a little bit in one of my books which says: 'Oh, mine own land, oceans and leagues away and still near to me. Oh my land of dock and nettles and scutty little mounds. My land of stones, high stones, round stones, keep old, keep wise, wear the mantle of your years. Do not let young men, young marauders or foreign mercenaries procure you.'

And I feel very strongly about it. I am often asked, and perhaps maybe slightly criticised about why I don't live there, and the reason why I don't live there - I think I've come to understand it - is a very simple one, that it has such a strong effect on me, such a heady effect on me and an upsetting effect on me that I have to be away from it in order to get any perspective at all for writing.

DONNCHA: County Clare obviously has very much to do with your being a writer?

EDNA: Yes, I would think so, though I'm sure that a writer is born like maybe a person with a harelip is born or a singer is born; but the background into which you are born decides, so to speak, the colour of your writing. If I had been born an urban woman then I would have written in a different way about different things. As we all know, and finally realise, it is our first impressions - and I mean real things, the things that impress themselves into us - that give us the rhythm and the habit and the predilections for our later life.

DONNCHA: did you write much when you were young and going to school in Clare?

EDNA: Well, I loved writing. I always did and still do. I write aloud. I write, actually, I think - this may sound a little bit vain - I write to be read aloud. I love the mesmer of incantation and incantatory prose, and when I was going to school we got essays and I loved that. I was so excited about doing those things that I would sit down coming home along the road and do little bits and then walk on further and then sit down, cross that out and do another little bit. It was my utter joy and it was, in a funny way, almost like my religion. I mean, I also read and said a lot of prayers. I loved beautiful prayers, Latin prayers. I loved the language of 'My soul doth magnify the Lord and my spirit hath rejoiced in God, my Saviour.'

DONNCHA: The incantatory quality?

EDNA: Yes. I don't like boring, modern, flat, dull things.

*   *   *

DONNCHA: How did your family feel about your early writing?

EDNA: I think that they are, in a very strange way, almost detached from it. I mean, that sounds hard to believe, but I think they are, because they don't talk about it much and they certainly don't in any way castigate me.

DONNCHA: Was there any writing in your family?

EDNA: No, there was no actual writing but I realise from listening to him that my father was a really compulsive storyteller. He has that ability which very few people have for telling a story well. You know, no matter how well I understand its unfolding and its ending I have often asked him to tell me the same story over and over again.

DONNCHA: What did you read as a child?

EDNA: We had those English schoolbooks in which there were

extracts from everything. Ruskin, I remember reading a bit of Ruskin's *Stories of Venice,* and Thoreau, who was very beautiful about ice and frost, and the thing which made the deepest impression on me, apart from prayerbooks, was the reading of Irish poems and myths. I loved all those stories of the Fianna and all the early poems in Irish and in English.

DONNCHA: You were writing, of course, out of a great Clare culture, a traditional type of culture with a great depth of history and folklore.

EDNA: Well, unfortunately when you're young you don't take sufficient interest in things. Yet I believe - going back to the magic - I believe in the vibrations. It was not so much that I had cultural experience; well, let's face it, it wasn't a very cultural experience. There was more power and magic in my environment than literature and I liked that. I would as a writer have liked or wanted to grow up in a literary family. I grew up in an ordinary soil from a fairly dark family. But writing does not come out of literature. It's like a cul-de-sac then. It's like incest. It doesn't work.

* * *

DONNCHA: And the day then came when you decided to be a writer. How did that come about?

EDNA: It's always hard to delineate the moment when one says, this is it! I've always wanted to be a writer. I still do. Before you publish something, you think maybe you want to be a writer and then having achieved that, you know that is what you want to be.

DONNCHA: Do you enjoy being known, being famous?

EDNA: No. I don't actually derive any pleasure from being known, being famous, or slightly famous or, indeed, slightly infamous! Each book that I finish - and I'll come back to your question in a minute - brings me into a kind of darker circle of my own psyche, my own imagination and it's in it that I'm interested. I have just finished *Night,* and, you know, I feel shredded. I couldn't think of anything only of making it perfect.

As for the actual practical thing, I used to write short pieces for the *Irish Press* - quite bad I think, because I wrote very extravagantly. I didn't have much what you call spareness. And then I met an English publisher who came to see the man to whom I was married at that time and he, the publisher, was from Hutchinson; he suggested that they would pay me £25 [advance], which they did, to write a novel and the novel was *The Country Girls*. I remember receiving the £25 - I spent it immediately, and having spent it, I thought, Oh my God, I now must write the book!

I wrote it the first month after I left Ireland. I left in November 1959 on Guy Fawkes Day and it was finished before Christmas. I just wrote it. I can safely say I take no credit for it, it wrote itself. You know the phrase - when they say it was given to you. It was given to me.

DONNCHA: Your 'country girls' were very real to you obviously?

EDNA: Very real. Still are, but, you know, it was a younger period. It's like looking at an old photograph. You think, did I look like that, or, did I write like that? Very real to me, but then, in a funny way, everything that I experience - for instance my own children now are very real to me. I mean really real, even in their absence. I can't have any relationships that aren't real. Though I live in a semi-fantasy there is a kind of terrible reality in me too or a longing for a reality.

DONNCHA: How real is Ireland to you?

EDNA: Very! I don't have any other reality. For instance, I've written about being 'Among the Brits, the painted people, a land where the King had piles.' What am I doing here? I'm not hiding. I'm almost like somebody who goes into a cave, or a wood, or a monastery. I'm working in conditions that seem to suit me.

Biography

Edna O'Brien's first book, *The Country Girls,* (1959) was immediately banned by the Irish Censorship Board. This seemed to signal the course her career would take, always attracting publicity, much of it unfavourable. With her next two books, *The Lonely Girl,* (1962) and *Girls In Their Married Bliss,* (1964), which were also banned, she completed a trilogy in which a country girl finds maturity through disappointment in love. Her fourth and fifth novels, *August is a wicked Month,* (1965) and *Casualties Of Peace,* (1966) suffered the seemingly inevitable banning. Not alone were her first five novels banned; a parish priest in her native county of Clare bought her books in bulk and burned them publicly.

Edna O'Brien was born on 15 December 1930 in Tomgraney, Co. Clare, daughter of a farmer who was a member of the Old IRA. She was educated at the National School in Scariff, the Convent of Mercy in Loughrea and the Pharmaceutical College in Dublin. In 1951 she married Ernest Gebler; the marriage was dissolved in 1964. She has two sons, Carlos and Sasha. She moved to London in 1959 and still lives there but makes frequent visits to Ireland.

Those are the essential biographical details. A close study of her writings brings one nearer to the woman behind them, although it would be an error to regard them as autobiographical. Like most writers, she draws on her experience of life to create and populate the world of her imagination. It is a world inimical to women, a male-dominated society in which women need all their courage and fortitude to survive. *The Country Girls,* and to a lesser degree, its successors in the trilogy, record an innocence and naivety which has charmed many readers. Her later novels are darker and more sombre in tone and atmosphere; life has become harsher; loss, loneliness and defeat stalk through their pages.

She has been very successful. Known and admired as an Irish beauty, she has been interviewed and photographed many times by the popular press. Literary critics tend to class her as a popular novelist. Popular she certainly is, but it is unlikely that she would have been included in the studies of Irish writers published by the Bucknell University Press, along with Frank O'Connor, Francis Stuart, Brian Moore and others, if her work had not more strength and depth than is implied by the adjective 'popular'. The truth is that she is a born writer, with a narrative power that makes her novels compulsively readable.

The Lonely Girl was adapted by her for the screen under the title *The Girl with Green Eyes*. She wrote a screenplay *Zee and Co.*, which was published in book form in 1971, and then filmed in 1972 as *X, Y and Zee,* starring Elizabeth Taylor. Her major non-fiction works are *Mother Ireland,* (1976), her own highly personal version of Irish history, and *Arabian Days* (1978), an account of a visit to the Middle East. In 1974 her play *The Gathering* was presented at the Abbey Theatre and received an unmerciful drubbing from the home critics.

Edna O'Brien did not want to write easy, cosy stories. She asked questions about the family and about love, disturbing questions. Love is a dominant theme in her work, a love far removed from the starry-eyed raptures of romantic novels. An Irish critic has summed her up as 'a natural writer with an absolutely Irish turn of phrase and style of humour, tart and generous, gentle and sly.'

Acknowledgements

The publishers thank the following for permission to use photographs: the National Library pp 8, 83; *The Irish Times* pp 55, 79, 140; RTE pp 60, 63; the *Irish Press* p. 42; Fergus Bourke p. 36; G.A. Duncan pp 108, 132; Bill St. Leger p. 51; C. Carson, Derry, p. 124; the *Western People* p. 116; Síghle Bn. Uí Dhonnchadha p. 91; ITGWU p. 86.